20th-century ceramics

PAUL ATTERBURY *CONSULTANT*

ANTIQUES CHECKLIST

General Editor: Frankie Leibe

MILLER'S ANTIQUES CHECKLIST:
20th-century Ceramics

Consultant: Paul Atterbury
General Editor: Frankie Leibe

First published in Great Britain in 2003 by Miller's,
a division of Mitchell Beazley,
both imprints of
Octopus Publishing Group Ltd.
2–4 Heron Quays
Docklands
London E14 4JP

Miller's is a registered trademark of Octopus Publishing Group Ltd.

Senior Executive Editor	Anna Sanderson
Executive Art Editor	Rhonda Fisher
Project Editor	Rosemary Amos
Project & Jacket Designer	Victoria Bevan
Page Layout	Louise Griffiths
Indexer	Sue Farr
Proofreader	Catherine Blake
Production	Angela Couchman

Set in Caslon 540, Caslon 224 bold and Caslon 3
Produced by Toppan Printing Co., (HK) Ltd.
Printed and bound in China

Jacket: *Beswick Zebra-striped Ware, 1950s*
Half-title page: *Refrigerator ware by Hall China, 1940s (see p.142)*

Freeform vase by Poole Pottery c.1958

CONTENTS

ART POTTERY

STUDIO POTTERY

ARTIST CERAMICS

BRITISH CERAMICS

NORTH AMERICAN CERAMICS

CONTINENTAL CERAMICS

GLOSSARY 183

BIBLIOGRAPHY 185

INDEX 186

PICTURE CREDITS 191

HOW TO USE THIS BOOK

Although there are numerous excellent and informative books on the subject of antiques – and in particular twentieth-century ceramics – many novice collectors still feel hesitant when it comes to actually purchasing an item. Collectors need to learn the technique of interrogating a piece to find out what it is and whether it is genuine.

The *20th-century Ceramics* Antiques Checklist will show you how to assess a piece as an expert would, and provides checklists of questions you should ask before making a purchase. The answer to most (if not all) of the questions should be "yes", but remember there are always exceptions to the rule: if in doubt, seek expert guidance.

An overview of Art Pottery sets the scene for the 20thC, and is followed by a brief look at the key exponents of Studio Pottery and Artist Ceramics. The bulk of the book covers factory-produced ceramics. These are organized by factory, designer, or collecting niche. A glossary and a bibliography are at the back of the book.

Treat the book as a knowledgeable companion, and discover that collecting is a matter of experience, and of asking the right questions.

Each double-page spread looks at items belonging to a particular factory, designer, or category of collecting.

The first page shows a carefully chosen representative item of a type that can usually be found at antiques stores or auction houses (rather than only in museums).

The caption gives the date of the piece shown, and a code for the price of this type of article.

A checklist of questions gives you the key to recognizing, dating, and authenticating pieces of the type shown.

BURGESS & LEIG

Golf jug by Burgess & Leigh c.1930s; value code F

Identification checklist for Burleigh Ware Sporting jugs
1. Is it made of earthenware?
2. Is it an eccentric shape?
3. Is it hand-painted?
4. Does it depict a sporting activity – tennis cricket – that was popular in the 1930s?
5. Does it have black painted dots on the r
6. Does it have a Burleigh Ware mark on t

Burgess & Leigh
Established in 1862 in Burslem, Staffordshire, from 1877 the company traded as Burgess & Leigh, making a range of underglaze decorated earthenware tablewares,

kitchenwares, and in traditional style the company was tableware patterns coordinate with t salad sets. From th production was ma Ware (see p.55).

Jugs
In the 1930s the c launched a range painted jugs that w popular at the tim eagerly collected t
* Examples in typ colours such as yel collectable than th muted tones.
* The Animal jugs a range of different flamingos, kingfish

54

Useful background
information is
provided about the
craftsman, factory,
or type of ware.

The second page
shows you what
details to look for.

BURGESS & LEIGH

squirrels, rabbits (on Harvest
jugs) monkeys, and dragons –
that either form the handle of
the jug (more collectable) or
decorate the body. Among the
rarest are the jugs with sloth
handles.
* The Parrot jugs, see below,
made c.1930s, are especially

flower patterns, and abstract
and geometric designs such as
Florentine, Sylvan and Garland,
with black tube-lining on white
grounds with blue-and-gold
patterns.
* Wares marked with Charlotte
Rhead's signature are eagerly
collected.

Later domestic wares
After post-war restrictions were
lifted, Burgess & Leigh
relaunched their domestic wares
in the 1950s with the Fantasia
range – a stylish interpretation
of the new contemporary look –
as seen on the sideplate shown
on p.54, made in 1959.
* Fantasia reflected the 1950s
fascination with graphic decoration featuring contemporary
domestic items, as seen also on
the Homemaker range produced
by Ridgway (see p.100).
* Designed by Harold Bennett,
it was produced in fashionable
black and white.
* Manchester City Museum
and Art Gallery commissioned a
reproduction issue of Fantasia
for commercial sale in the 1990s.
These later pieces have a
modern backstamp to distinguish
them from early originals.

In the 1990s, the company gave
traditional domestic ware forms
a new look using a fresh
interpretation of the traditional
blue-and-white and all-over
chintzware patterns on the
Calico kitchenware range, and
the newly fashionable, revived
traditional decorative techniques
of stencilling and sponging on
tea and coffee wares.

Information helps
you to detect
fakes, copies, and
reproductions.

Hints and tips help
you to assess factors
that affect value – for
example, condition
and availability.

Further photographs
show:
* items in a different
style by the same
craftsman or factory
* similar, but perhaps
less valuable wares
that may be mistaken
for the more
collectable type
* common variations
on the piece shown
in the main picture
* similar wares by
other craftsmen
* the range of shapes
or decorative motifs
associated with a
particular factory
or period.

H

, golf,

m?
he base?

dinnerware
. By the 1920s
roducing
en suite to
, fruit, and
e 1930s,
rked Burleigh

mpany
f hand-
ere hugely
and are
day.
cally Art Deco
low are more
ose in more

feature
animals –
es, parrots,

popular and form a separate
collecting niche as no two are
the same.
* Sporting jugs are another
collecting niche. Again, no two
are the same, and in general,
those with more individual detail
– such as the checked trousers
shown on the Golf jug in the
main picture left, rather than
plain trousers seen on other
versions – are more popular.

Charlotte Rhead
A major coup, announced in
press advertisements, was the
arrival of the distinguished
designer Charlotte Rhead (see
p.127), who worked for Burgess
& Leigh from 1926–31 and
produced many new patterns for
ornamental and functional wares.
* Early Rhead designs appear
under the Burleigh mark and
were applied to shapes already in
production.
* Later Rhead designed both
new shapes and patterns.
* Designs include fruit-and-

55

Marks and signatures
are explained.

change in rate, adjust the dollar
value accordingly.
The codes are as follows:
A £20,000+ ($30,000+)
B £15–20,000 ($22,500–30,000)
C £10–15,000 ($15–22,500)

D £5–10,000 ($7,500–15,000)
E £2–5,000 ($3–7,500)
F £1–2,000 ($1,500–3,000)
G £500–1,000 ($750–1,500)
H £250– £500 ($375–750)
I £1–250 (under $375)

DESIGN HISTORY

At the beginning of the 20thC, many ceramic designs still looked back to the traditions of the 19thC. In Britain and the US hand-crafted Arts and Crafts-inspired art pottery was in vogue, alongside Neo-classical Revival styles. By the 1910s, ceramics were beginning to reflect the influence of both the French and Belgian European Art Nouveau styles. Other ceramicists experimented with Oriental-influenced shapes, glazes, and lustres.

In the 1920s the reaction to the horrors of WW I could be seen in the determinedly hedonistic Jazz Age with an emphasis on fantasy and escapism, and exotic bright glazes with lustre finishes. The *Exposition des Arts Decoratifs et Industriels Modernes* in Paris in 1925 showcased the new Art Deco style, cool, elegant, and modern, with clean lines and brightly coloured hand-painted decoration inspired by abstract art.

During WWII and in the early 1940s, wartime restrictions dictated the plain, simple shapes of the monochromatic Utility wares.

The 1950s celebrated colour and pattern in a determination to create an exciting contemporary style that deliberately avoided historicism. American streamlined shapes and solid or two-tone colours were quickly copied by British manufacturers, who also adopted the abstract graphic, linear newly fashionable Scandinavian style. The application of lithographic printing meant that printed decoration was rapidly replacing hand-painted designs on commercial wares. The Festival of Britain in 1951 abounded with organic decorative motifs and forms drawn from a newfound optimism in the power of scientific progress.

By the 1960s this optimism took the form of increasingly bright colours, more geometric cylindrical forms, and psychedelic patterns, alongside the more restrained, understated "good taste" associated with the "less is more" philosophy of the Modern Movement.

By the 1970s the optimism of the 1960s was beginning to evaporate in the face of growing concerns about the environment. Preoccupations with conservion, self-sufficiency, and moving back to the land resulted in softer, earthy colours, textured surfaces, and patterns inspired by plants, flowers, and natural forms.

By the 1980s, increased spending on the home became part of the new ostentatious display of affluence. Decoration and pattern dominated form, with a revival of traditional techniques such as sponging and stencilling both for interiors and ceramics.

In the 1990s, the focus was on design, and the designer, as the quest for "individuality" was reflected in the desire for unique ceramics, and well-known names from a variety of disciplines were invited to design or endorse ranges for ceramic manufacturers.

1900 – 10

Shapes

Wide variety: traditional; Oriental; Neo-classical
Revival style; curving Art Nouveau forms, especially
vases; organic forms.

Colours

Wide range, usually muted blues, greens, white,
and cream; light, delicate Neo-classical colours; soft
or muted Art Nouveau shades.

Decoration

nd-painted, transfer-printed, tube-lined; floral
Neo-classical motifs; Art Nouveau motifs,
ic plant and foliage, or more linear and
ambé and iridescent lustre glazes.

ment; Neo-classical style of Robert
rt Nouveau; Chinese ceramics
itions and early cultures.

9

1920s

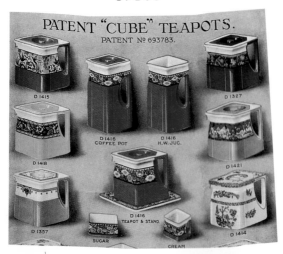

Shapes

Oriental, i.e. ginger jars and large vases; some early geometric straight-sided Art Deco forms; rounded forms.

Colours

Blue, red, yellow, pink, orange; rich blue and dark red on lustre wares; rich reds and browns on flambé wares; striking Art Deco combinations of red, black, gold, and green.

Decoration

Hand-painted, transfer-printed; rich glaze effects and gilding on lustre wares; stylized floral patterns; abstract banded and dotted patterns.

Influences

Rich ornament of early French Art Deco style; Orie… wares; fairyland and fantasy landscapes; Ancient E… Cubism and the Modern Movement.

1930s–40s

Shapes

Geometric forms – square plates, conical cups, triangular handles; elegant minimalist architectural forms; streamlined organic tableware.

Colours

Bright, vivid colours: black, red, yellow, orange, brown, green; off-whites, celadon, pale yellow, pale grey.

Decoration

Hand-painted; transfer-printed: abstract geometric motifs; small repeat abstract patterns; floral patterns, including chintzware; solid monochromatic matt glazes; incised lines.

Influences

European Modern Movement; contemporary abstract art; organic design exhibitions; Jazz; textiles.

1 9 5 0 s

Shapes

Rounded, organic and streamlined tableware, coupé plates; angular, stylized ornaments; novelty shapes.

Colours

Pastels and natural colours; muted two-tones; black and white, often with contrasting primary colours.

Decoration

Largely litho-printed, some hand-painted; patterns: small, abstract, plaid; motifs: foreign travel, food, popular music.

Influences

Scandinavian design; Christian Dior's "New Look"; foreign travel and food; casual entertaining; American streamlining, new consumer goods; modern sculpture.

1960s

Shapes

Tall, straight-sided cylinders, especially tall coffee pots with flat lids; straight-sided dishes and bowls.

Colours

Primary colours; tangerine, purple, blue, and green, orange, and brown; muted Scandinavian neutrals.

Decoration

Mostly litho-printed; patterns: large, bold abstract; inspired by contemporary art movements; psychedelic; "flower-power"-inspired florals.

Influences

Op Art, Pop Art, psychedelia, youth culture and Carnaby Street, Scandinavian interior design and textiles, studio-potters' hand-finished look.

1970s

Shapes

Softened versions of cylinder shape, with curvaceous handles and rounded lids; more rounded forms; traditional "rustic" oven-to-table ware forms.

Colours

More earthy palette: various shades of brown, orange, green, rust; two-tone wares.

Decoration

Screen-printed patterns; textured surfaces; softer patterns incorporating natural flora and fauna; ethnic patterns; colours, patterns, and motifs that reflect the natural environment.

Influences

"Back-to-the-land" and self-sufficiency movements in the face of growing environmental concerns; "New Age" preoccupation with ethnic cultures and ancient sites and monuments.

1980s – 90s

Shapes

Little dramatic innovation: a variety of traditional and more innovative softer forms as the emphasis switched from shape to novel decoration and surface pattern.

Colours

Wide variety of colours: softer colours for traditional floral patterns; dramatic contrasting colour for abstract designs.

Decoration

Revival of traditional sponging and stencilling techniques for both traditional and modern patterns; all-over textile-inspired patterns reminiscent of chintzware; Laura Ashley-style florals; abstract coordinated patterns.

Influences

Ostentatious display and conspicuous consumption of the 1980s as manifested in patterns.

ART POTTERY

Illustrations of the Iris glaze, Rookwood Pottery catalogue (1904)

The art pottery produced in Britain from c.1866 and in the US from c.1880 into the 20thC was largely inspired by the ideals and followers of the Arts and Crafts Movement. In the face of increased mass-production and mechanization, hand-crafted or individually designed or decorated pieces by such leading Arts and Crafts designers as William De Morgan and Christopher Dresser were at a premium, and art pottery became so popular that large manufacturers introduced their own, more affordable, lines. A fascination with early Chinese and Turkish ceramics led to experiments with new coloured glaze effects, including exotic lustres, that resulted in important technical advances; a preoccupation with other non-Western cultures introduced unusual forms; and a return to decoration based on animals, flora, and fauna all laid the ground for the new styles, including Art Nouveau and Art Deco, that were to become popular in the early 20thC.

Britain

From the late 19thC there was a flourishing and widespread Art Pottery Movement in Britain, where small and large manu-facturers produced their own ranges, often drawing on the talents of established Arts and Crafts designers.

Longboat vase (c.1908) by Bernard Moore

The success of art pottery encouraged leading manu-facturers to develop their own lines: Minton & Co. set up the short-lived (1871–75) Minton Art Pottery Studios in Kensington Gore in order to establish links with students from the nearby National Training School; Doulton & Co. (est. 1815) used profits from its stoneware domestic and sanitary wares to set up an art pottery that estab-lished links with the nearby Lambeth School of Art, resulting from c.1870 in a highly successful range of salt-glazed hand-thrown stoneware that was

16

decorated in subdued colours by such notable designers as Florence Barlow and George Tinworth. The far smaller pottery of the Martin Brothers, set up in Fulham, in 1873 and relocating to Southall in 1877, became well-known for its range of highly individualistic salt-glazed stoneware, in particular the now highly collectable birds and grotesques.

Art pottery was produced in many regions of Britain. Christopher Dresser, who had worked for Minton & Co. in Stoke-on-Trent, provided designs for an inventive range of forms for the Linthorpe Pottery (1879–89) near Middlesborough, then managed by Henry Tooth, who later, together with William Ault, set up the Bretby Art Pottery (1883–1990) in Derbyshire, which was one of the more adventurous small manufacturers known for its art vases, in myriad colours and shapes drawn from all over the world, as shown in the advertisement below. The Della Robbia Pottery (1894–1906) in Birkenhead, near Liverpool, produced hand-thrown pots, usually in organic forms with all-over decoration in lead glazes in muted colours. Those by well-known designers such as Liz Wilkins are pre-eminently collectable. At Barnstaple, Devon, in 1879, C. H. Brannam established a pottery that from the 1880s produced a popular range of Barum artware (see p.72). In Bridgend, Glamorgan, the Ewenny Pottery (est. c.1800) developed a popular range of puzzle jugs and dishes with coloured glazes and *sgraffito* decoration.

Advertisement c.1921 from The Pottery Gazette *for Bretby Ware.*

Bretby "NERTON" Ware.

Bretby "CARVED BAMBOO" Ware.

Much British art pottery was produced by individual potters, many of whom were inspired by early Chinese pottery. From the 1880s, Bernard Moore had been researching the superb glazes used on early Chinese pots. From 1905, using bought-in blanks, he experimented with Oriental and Middle Eastern glazes, flambés, lustres, and other effects, in particular the *sang-de-boeuf* glazes for which he is best known. These rich red glazes were used as grounds for figural hand-painted decoration, often in gold, of exotic motifs, as seen on the Longboat vase (bottom, p.16). At the Ruskin Pottery (est. 1898, Birmingham), William Howson Taylor used a white body in Chinese-inspired forms that were primarily vehicles for experiments with high-fired abstract coloured-glaze effects. These leadless glazes and colours ranged from broken colours, to combinations of several colours through to extraordinarily rich jewel-like hues, that reached their apogee in the Real Flambé Ware, such as the large vase, above. From

Flambé vase and stand (c.1925) by Ruskin Pottery

1882, the highly influential and prolific potter William De Morgan decorated tiles and pots with bluish-grey gold and ruby-red lustre glazes inspired by Hispano-Moresque wares, and from 1888 established his own pottery in London, where he experimented with double and triple lustre effects. A passion for glaze effects was also the driving force behind much of the Royal Lancastrian art pottery, such as the vase below produced by Pilkington's Tile & Pottery Co. (est. c.1891, near Manchester), where William Burton, previously employed at Wedgwood's, developed a range of new glazes, including opalescent and lustre effects. The designer and illustrator Walter Crane produced decorative designs for Pilkington's, and for other reputable ceramics firms such as Maws & Co. (1850–1967).

Royal Lancastrian vase (1932) by Pilkington's Tile & Pottery Co.

North America

Production of art pottery in the United States began following the Centennial Exhibition in Philadelphia, Pennsylvania, in 1876. The utilitarian wares needed to settle a new continent had done their work, and Americans were now ready to decorate their new homes. Inspired by the decorative Japanese-influenced European ceramics seen at the exhibition, in 1880 Maria Longworth Nichols set up the Rookwood Pottery (est. Cincinnati, Ohio, 1880) that was to lead the field with a range of high-quality wares with hand-painted naturalistic decoration and

*Vessels (after 1920) by
Van Briggle Pottery*

superb, mostly glossy, glazes. The earlier Standard Glaze wares featured flowers, animals, and (more rare and now highly collected), Native American Indians. Other highly successful lines included Vellum Ware, with a soft matt glaze, and Iris Ware (see top p.16), the latter with a superb clear glossy finish that helped the company win a gold medal at the Paris *Exposition* of 1900.

The Roseville and Weller potteries in nearby Zanesville, Ohio, competed fiercely both with each other and Rookwood. Roseville, established in 1890 for the production of utilitarian stoneware, began artware production c.1900. While initially largely producing less expensive copies of Rookwood lines, such as the hand-decorated Rozane Ware, by 1905 Roseville had introduced several successful original lines, such as Della Robbia (designed by the English potter Frederick Hurten Rhead, a former Weller designer), Fudji, and Crystallis. Mass-produced artware was introduced c.1914, and this production ware is now among the most keenly collected pieces of the most widely collected of American art potteries. The Weller Pottery (see p.132) initially imitated the Rookwood production with its range of Lonhuda Ware, later renamed Louwelsa. The success of these middle-range artwares led Weller to introduce many new lines of earthenwares with coloured slips, as well as, briefly, an iridescent glaze.

There were two major strands in American art pottery: hand-painting decorative designs onto ready-made blanks in the Victorian tradition; and carved and moulded forms in which form and decoration were conceived as a whole. While the Ohio Valley potteries largely adhered to the first strand, other areas of production mixed the two. At the Grueby Pottery in Boston, Massachusetts, New England, William Grueby (1867–1925) was throwing organic pots, many with hand-carved floral designs, with distinctive thick, opaque glazes, in particular, the matt green for which he is best known. However, the Boston Saturday Evening Girls Club, known as the Paul Revere Pottery from 1908, specialized in hand-painted decoration of farm animals.

In the Southern States, Newcomb College Pottery (act. 1895–1945) in New Orleans employed women to decorate pots hand-thrown by master potters. Favourite motifs included the flora and fauna of the local bayou region, usually in green or blue, with shiny glazes until c.1910, and subsequently soft matt glazes. At the Biloxi Pottery, Mississippi, from 1880 to c.1907 George Ohr, "the mad potter from Biloxi" (1857–1918), produced a prolific and extraordinary range of asymmetrical and unusual red earthenware forms, often with crimped or folded rims; early examples have bright, mottled lustrous glazes; later examples were unglazed.

The rich clay deposits of California attracted such distinguished potters as Frederick Hurten Rhead (1880–1942), who founded the Arequipa Pottery (1911–18). The pottery provided occupational therapy for women at the Arequipa TB Sanatorium, which produced bulbous forms with slip-trailed decoration of stylized flora. The warm dry climate of Colorado led Artus van Briggle, formerly employed as a decorator at Rookwood, to relocate there and open the Van Briggle Pottery in Colorado Springs in 1900. Here he continued work on a dead matt glaze that created a sensation at the *Exposition Universelle* in Paris in 1900 and produced a range of Art Nouveau-influenced slip-cast vases in which the figures appear to grow out of the vessel, notably the Lorelei vase, early versions of which are highly collectable. Early designs were produced for many years, although the colour palette and glaze application became more standardized (see above). Fakes are known– generally small with a black lustrous glaze.

STUDIO POTTERY

The 20thC Studio Pottery Movement can be seen as a reaction against standardized manufactured ceramics. Individual potters preferred to work in isolation, or with like-minded others, as independent craftsmen, producing unique one-off hand-made and hand-decorated pieces characterized by spontaneity, in the tradition of the folk potters. In Britain, the Movement was primarily craft-based, with many potters concerned with reviving traditional techniques. Potters in continental Europe shared the British preoccupation with the disappearing folk traditions of functional pottery but also responded to the influence of the Modern Movement, often producing more austere forms that influenced commercial ceramics, and were often happy to work within industry. In the US, by contrast, there was little nostalgia for dying traditions, and young studio potters looked to contemporary art movements or reused historical motifs in a deliberately ironic way.

In Britain, Bernard Leach is seen as the father of the 20thC Studio Pottery Movement. He and his followers dominated the field until the 1950s, emphasizing the need for functional hand-made domestic wares alongside one-off individual studio pieces. Their emulated Chinese and Japanese glazes became part of the studio pottery repertory, along with free-hand brush-painted or slip-trailed decoration.

At the outbreak of WWII, a number of key European potters emigrated either to the United States or to Britain. Lucie Rie and Hans Coper were influenced by the Modern Movement and contemporary sculpture. They emphasized exact and controlled forms rather than spontaneity, glazes rather than hand-painted or trailed decoration, and influenced a generation of British potters both through their own work and their teaching.

The young British potters who trained in the art colleges from the 1960s were increasingly freed from the constraints of function and form, and there was a move towards ever more abstract, often hand-built, sculptural ceramics, whose decoration was inspired by sculpture from ancient cultures, abstract painting, the work of Picasso, or even music, rather than historical precedent. The Royal College of Art, London, in particular, provided a fertile training ground, where students were taught by Hans Coper and other distinguished sculptors and ceramicists.

In the US, the acceptance from the mid-1940s of ceramics as an art form and academic discipline rather than a craft was due in part to the influence of European ceramicists and teachers. As a result American studio potters were influenced by the ideas and styles of such major 20thC movements as Abstract Expressionism, Pop Art and Post-Modernism, and in turn influenced studio potters in Britain and continental Europe.

A Tree of Life dish, by Bernard Leach, with slip decoration 1923; value code E.

Identification checklist for Bernard Leach slipware

1. Is the piece influenced by medieval English pottery and slipware?
2. Is it thickly potted in earthenware?
3. Is the form simple and traditional?
4. Is the decoration pictorial?
5. Is the decoration drawn in raised clay or slip?
6. Does it have a BL seal?

Bernard Leach (1887–1979)

Leach originally trained in London as a graphic artist. In 1909 he visited Japan, where he became interested in Oriental ceramics and learned the craft from some of the most distinguished potters in Japan. In 1920 Leach returned to England, and established a pottery in St Ives, Cornwall, that provided a training ground for some of the leading figures of the English Studio Pottery Movement of which Leach is considered to be the father. Leach was also a talented artist, author of the influential ceramic treatise *A Potter's Book*, and respected teacher, whose many students helped to create the "Leach" School.

Slipware

This traditional technique was used in Britain from the medieval period, but was at its peak in the early 17thC. The earthenware pot is dipped into white slip and extra details are added by trailing, dotting and combing other russet or chocolate-coloured slips on to the body. The piece is then coated in a thick lead glaze that turns white clay yellow when fired.

An interest in Eastern philosophy and a fascination with the Japanese artist/craftsman tradition inspired much of Leach's early work. He also had a deep love of medieval English pottery and managed to fuse the two traditions, acting as a bridge between East and West.

BERNARD LEACH II

A "Leaping Salmon" vase by Bernard Leach c.1970; value code C

Identification checklist for Bernard Leach post-war pots
1. Is the piece made of porcelain or stoneware?
2. Is the decoration more discreet and less pictorial than in earlier pieces?
3. Do the shape and decoration reflect Oriental models?
4. Is the decoration brush drawn?
5. Are the glazes subtly coloured or textured?
6. Does the piece have a BL seal?

Decoration
* Most wares are brown, cream, celadon, grey, ochre, brownish-black, or a combination of these.
* Popular painted motifs included leaping salmon, the wandering pilgrim, the flying bird, and the running hare.
* Other decorative techniques include inlay, *sgraffito*, wax resist, stencils, trailing, combing, and fluting.
* From the mid-1960s many of Leach's pots were decorated with cut and fluted sides, and deeply engraved or coarsely furrowed lines.

* Leach designed many tablewares for larger-scale production at St Ives by students and assistants.

Marks
* Most Leach pots are marked.
* An impressed BL seal is used on pots that Leach threw and decorated himself.
* The St Ives monogram appears only on pieces fired in the St Ives kiln.
* Leach probably decorated a pot with a painted or incised monogram, but another potter threw it.

LEACH'S FOLLOWERS

A stoneware vase by Shoji Hamada
c.1955; value code F

Identification checklist for Shoji Hamada stonewares
1. Is the form Oriental?
2. Is it thickly potted?
3. Is the decoration free and spontaneous?
4. Is the decoration abstract, or does it include a bamboo spray?

Shoji Hamada (1891–1978)
Hamada met Leach in Japan in 1918 and came to England with him in 1920 to set up the St Ives Pottery. In 1924 he returned to Japan, where he continued to produce pots that reflect Zen tenets of honesty, utility, humility, and repetition.
* Pots made at St Ives are marked with the St Ives monogram and the Japanese symbol for Shoji; pots made after his return to Japan in 1924 are unmarked.

Leach students
The first students included Michael Cardew (see p.24), Nora Braden (b.1901), and Katharine Pleydell-Bouverie (1895–1985). From 1928 to 1936 Braden and Pleydell-Bouverie shared a studio, where they experimented with ash glazes, as seen on the flared bowl left made by Braden in 1935.

Leach Standard ware
Original pieces by Leach are extremely expensive. More affordable are the production wares designed by Leach but made by the many apprentices at the St Ives Pottery. By the early 1950s, the Leach studio potters were producing over 70 different glazed stoneware designs. Leach's children and grand-children have become well-known potters, working in a similar style.

MICHAEL CARDEW

*"Bird-dish" by Michael Cardew
c.1930, value code G*

Identification checklist for slipwares by Michael Cardew

1. Is the piece earthenware?
2. Is it hand-thrown?
3. Is the decoration spontaneous and original?
4. Does it feature an animal, bird, or fish?
5. Is the surface decorated with trailed slip or scratched design?
6. Is the form bold and robust?

Michael Cardew (1901–82)
Cardew was one of Bernard Leach's first and most distinguished pupils. After training with him at St Ives in the 1920s, he started potteries at Winchcombe, Gloucestershire in 1926 and at Wenford Bridge, near Bodmin, Cornwall in 1939. A skilled thrower, here he made functional pieces in lead-glazed earthenware inspired by old English traditions. Following a visit to Africa in 1942 he produced brightly coloured stoneware. From 1949 he travelled between the two countries, researching, writing, lecturing, and potting and is considered a key figure in 20thC art pottery. Other members of the Cardew family also became potters.

Wares
* A huge range of domestic earthenware slipware in traditional forms, including vases, jugs, cider flagons, bottles, bowls, plates, chargers, teapots, dishes, and oil-lamps.
* 1930s pots decorated with motifs of animals, birds, and stags are very collectable.
* From 1942, African-influenced stonewares glazed in dark green with flashes of red iron, and blue-grey.

Glazes
* Early slipwares: a lead glaze made from lead sulphide that produces a rich chestnut brown and golden honey-yellow.
* 1930s: a black vitreous glaze.

Decoration
* Abstract designs and freely drawn animals.
* Trailed or scratched designs.

Marks
* Impressed MC seal.
* Winchcombe pieces: impressed MC seal and impressed combined W and P.
* St Ives monogram with impressed MC or MAC.

LUCIE RIE

Conical porcelain vase by Dame Lucie Rie
c.1964, value code E

Identification checklist for porcelain by Dame Lucie Rie
1. Is the form elegant and refined?
2. Is the style contemporary or sculptural?
3. Is the foot well-finished?
4. Is the decoration simple and restrained?
5. Does it have a distinctive glaze?
6. Is there an impressed "LR" seal on the base?

Dame Lucie Rie (1902–95)
Born in Vienna where she studied with the celebrated architect and designer Josef Hoffmann (1870–1956). Lucie Rie was already an acclaimed and accomplished potter when she and her husband came to England in 1938 after Hitler annexed Austria. Her husband moved to the United States in 1939 but Rie stayed in London, where she set up her own studio, becoming a British citizen in 1945. Initially she had to make buttons and tablewares to help finance her experiments in more artistic pottery, but she continued to make a range of highly distinctive, elegant, and refined pots, constantly experimenting with forms, glazes, and colours. From 1948 she began to work increasingly with porcelain and stoneware. Her work has influenced generations of potters and is among the most highly respected and sought-after of 20thC ceramics.

Style
Rie's distinctive pots are characterized by clean and elegant forms; distinctive, and often daring use of colour, texture; and the absence of figurative or patterned brushwork.

Marks
* From the early 1950s Rie's ceramics bore an impressed LR seal.
* The seals changed over time and the different styles can be used to date the pieces.

LUCIE RIE & HANS COPER

Stoneware globular pot by Hans Coper
c.1953; value code E

Identification checklist for stoneware by Hans Coper
1. Does the piece have a distinctive, sometimes idiosyncratic, perhaps machine-age, form?
2. Does it have a textured surface?
3. Does it have a monochrome colour scheme?
4. Does it have an impressed HC seal?
5. Does it feature coloured clays?
6. Are the forms predominantly sculptural?

Hans Coper (1920–81)

A refugee from Saxony, in 1946 Hans Coper joined Lucie Rie's studio as an assistant in her button factory. He showed such application that Rie encouraged him to train further, introduced him to her potting techniques, and the pair began a lifelong friendship and a collaboration that lasted for some 12 years. Coper set up his own London studio in 1959, and then moved to a farmhouse near Frome, Wiltshire. He was a highly influential teacher at Camberwell School of Art and the Royal College of Art and produced a range of fine pots until his early death. Coper was a perfectionist and destroyed any pots he thought unsatisfactory.

Domestic wares

Lucy Rie had produced a range of domestic ware in Vienna before she came to England. These early Rie pots, such as the teapot shown top p.27, are marked "LRG Wien" – her maiden name was Gompertz. Made of earthenware, they depend on elegant and finely potted forms, and the warmth of their surfaces, rather than decoration, for appeal. This focus on elegant forms and minimal decoration also characterizes the domestic wares that Rie and Coper made together.
* On early domestic wares made in Britain, such as the stoneware cups and saucers, bowl, and matching jugs shown right, made

c.1958, Coper threw the forms and Rie decorated them.
* These collaborative pieces will have both artists' seals and are very collectable.

Sgrafitto

Rie began using *sgrafitto* decoration following a visit in the late 1940s to Avebury Museum, Wiltshire, where she saw pots decorated with patterns scratched into the surface of the glaze with bird bones. From the early 1950s she began to use the technique on her own pots, using a needle to scratch through the glaze to the body before firing to create a network of finely hatched lines.

Forms and decoration

Both Rie and Coper experimented constantly with new forms. Rie tended to be influenced more by the natural world and endlessly explored the bowl form. Coper's forms were inspired by abstract art and modern sculpture.

* Rie: simple, elegant forms; flared conical bowls; tall bottle-shaped vases with flared lips; porcelain wares often have *sgraffito* decoration or may have simple bands of applied colour; inlay and fluting.
* Coper: unusual, idiosyncratic shapes created by the meticulous joining together of elements thrown on the wheel, often inspired by abstract art, modern painting, and sculpture; some early work is small-scale, later work includes monumental-size vases in "thistle", "poppy", and "spade" shapes; last works from 1970s, known as Cycladics, often arrow-head shape, are smaller and are eagerly collected.

Colour and glazes

The disparity in forms is also reflected in the disparity of Rie and Coper's use of colour. Coper used mainly monochrome colour schemes; muted creams, light browns, and black. Rie employed a wide range of colour, especially after 1948, when she installed an electric kiln and was able to experiment with high-fired stoneware and porcelain and new glazes.
* Coper: mainly monochrome colour schemes; light and dark glazes, almost completely matt.
* Rie: bold use of colour and texture, a huge variety of coloured clays, sometimes combined to create a swirled, marbled effect, and glazes, including lead, dark blue, light blue, pink, green, and a distinctive uranium yellow.
* Rie and Coper: glazes often used to produce distinctive thick, pitted textured surfaces.

ENGLISH

*A "Floating Particles" vase by Elizabeth Fritsch
c.1985; value code E.*

**Identification checklist for Elizabeth Fritsch
stoneware**
1. Does the piece have hand-painted decoration
in coloured slip?
2. Is the form elegant, possibly slightly flattened?
3. Is the decoration geometric and abstract?
4. Does the decoration create optical illusions of
space and perspective?
5. Are the colours subtle and harmonious?
6. Does it have a matt finish?

"New ceramics"
In the 1970s a "new ceramics"
group emerged from the Royal
College of Art, London. They
explored hand-building rather
than throwing, experimented
with the abstract concept of the
vessel, and often used pots as
a canvas on which to create
abstract designs.

Elizabeth Fritsch (b.1940)
Elizabeth Fritsch (RCA
1967–70) developed a range of
improvised stoneware vases,
bottles, and bowls with beautiful
hand-painted coloured slip
patterns that create extraordinary
spatial effects, often inspired by
science and music, as seen on

the vase in the main picture.
Many of her ceramics are
designed along themes and often
benefit from being shown in
small groups.

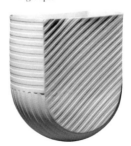

Elizabeth Fritsch is one of the most innovatory and influential of the new post-war group of studio potters.

Jacqui Poncelet (b.1947)
The work of Belgian-born Jacqueline Poncelet (RCA 1969–72) is highly collectible and falls into two distinct styles.
* Pre-mi-1970s she made small-scale bowls and vases (see

bottom p.28, made c.1972) in fine, almost translucent, bone-china cast in plaster moulds, with colour sometimes added to the mould or to the liquid slip.
* From c.1978 she made larger earthenware shapes – vases, dishes, and organic forms – with colourful decorative motifs.

Other important potters
Alison Britton (b.1948) experiments with the jug form and constructs architectural hand-built slab vessels from sheets of clay hand-painted with abstract designs. Her contemporary and fellow RCA graduate, Carol McNicholl (b.1943), makes hand-built ceramic objects, including bowls, vases, teapots,

etc, and the coffee set (1991) below, that make witty reference to traditional functional forms.
* Her slip-cast and assembled pieces have hand-painted decoration accentuating the shapes and forms within a piece.
* She produces both standard ware in series and unique studio pieces. The latter, signed underneath "Carol McNicholl", are the most collectable.
* From c.1980 Eileen Nisbet (1929–90) created elegant hand-built porcelain sculptural forms with minimal decoration. Her work, already found in museum collections, is increasingly popular with collectors but is highly priced.
* From the 1980s Ewen Henderson (1934–2000) made large-scale asymmetric non-functional rough-textured sculptural forms in muted colours, such as the large stoneware sack form (1990) shown left.
* More affordable is his range of smaller "teabowl" forms, which have similar qualities.
* From c.1979, Martin Smith made hand-thrown raku pots with precise forms and black and white geometric decoration; later work includes large hand-built red earthenware pots.
* Nicholas Homoky's (b.1950) polished porcelain bowls, cylinders, and vases have inlaid designs in black slip. Decoration is highly graphic, combining two-dimensional caricatures of traditional ceramic forms such as teapots on a three-dimensional form such as a bowl.

Collecting
* Contemporary studio ceramics is still a quite specialized area.
* Degree shows can be useful for spotting tomorrow's collectables.

Vase by Peter Voulkos
c.1954; value code E.

Identification checklist for Peter Voulkos ceramics
1. Is it a large-scale piece?
2. Does it have an original, perhaps hand-built, form?
3. Does it have muted or naturalistic colours?
4. Is it wheel-thrown, or does it have wheel-thrown elements?
5. Is it influenced by Abstract Expressionism?
6. Does it have an etched mark?

Influences
From 1945 American studio pottery was seen as an art form rather than a craft, and its influences were primarily contemporary art movements. In the 1940s distinguished immigrant potters such as Gertrud and Otto Natzler disseminated the influence and style of the European Modern Movement; in the 1950s other young American potters were inspired by home-grown Abstract Expressionism; from the 1960s California and the West Coast was the major centre for innovations. Pop Art, "Funk", and, later, Post Modernism, all influenced studio ceramics.

Peter Voulkos (b.1924)
Voulkos, who set up his own ceramics department at the Otis Art Institute, Los Angeles, in 1954, is seen as the father of American studio ceramics. He was the central figure of the new Ceramics Movement on the West Coast in the 1950s. His expressionistic, sculptural work is highly respected and collectable but is rarely found outside the US. His work falls into three main categories.
* Early pieces are finely potted, with light green and buff glazes, and virtually no surface texture or applied design.
* Middle-period pieces, such as the vase above, had rougher finishes and often included designs painted in the glaze.
* Late-period work is expressive, including huge assemblages of hand-built, hand-thrown pieces

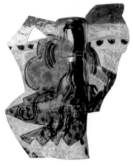

of clay inspired by themes such as the dish, the stack, or the vase, with rough-textured, blistered, dry surfaces.
* All Voulkos pieces are marked and many are also dated.

Gertrud and Otto Natzler
Although Gertrud (1908–71) and Otto Natzler (b.1908) studied briefly with a ceramicist in Vienna, their real education came through trial and error. In 1938, they emigrated to the US, where their technical accomplishment was highly influential. Their pots are collaborative: Gertrud threw the forms and Otto created the glazes.
* Their pieces, such as

the monumental vase shown here, made c.1962, typically have a fine profile and a distinctive, often textured, glaze.

Betty Woodman
Betty Woodman (b.1930) explores the vessel form, using historical ceramics as source

material for witty, irreverent pieces in bright colours in turn based on historical sources, such as the blue and white that was used on Italian majolica shown on the vase above (both sides illustrated), entitled Baroque Diptych and made 2001.
* Many of the pieces are earthenware, which allows for a wide range of glaze colours.
* The pieces are asymmetrical, hand-built and hand-painted in an exuberant freehand style, sometimes with different designs and colours on each side, as shown on the vase above.
* Many Woodman pieces have painterly titles, for example, *Still Life Vase No. 5*, which encompass the different elements of jug, vase, the painted decoration of flowers that it might contain, and the non-functional nature of the piece.
* Many Woodman pieces incorporate their own plinths as an ironic comment on the nature of displaying in museums.
* Woodman pieces are signed.

Collecting
* Form rather than colour is the key to collecting studio ceramics.
* If collecting a single piece by an artist, choose one that is representative of his or her mature style.
* If collecting a body of work by one artist, an unusual piece will add interest and value.
* Early pieces by major ceramicists are not necessarily more valuable than later pieces.
* It is essential to have proof of provenance for all important studio wares.
* Good condition is crucial to value: check carefully for restoration on vulnerable projecting areas.

EUROPEAN

*"Oxblood" glaze vase by Axel Salto
c.1937; value code F*

Identification checklist for Axel Salto ceramics
1. Is it a porcelain or stoneware vase?
2. Does it have an organic, often "prickly" shape, inspired by the natural world?
3. Does it have a tactile quality?
4. Does it have a distinctive coloured glaze?
5. Is it marked?

European studio potters
The different national styles and influences seen in commercial ceramics were often also seen in the work of European studio potters, many of whom produced both one-off studio pieces and also created designs for ceramic manufacturers.

Axel Salto (1889–1961)
One of Denmark's leading studio potters, Salto's work, like that of many Scandinavian ceramicists, was largely influenced by the natural world, with a distinctive "budding and sprouting" style inspired by plant forms, and highly incised and carved forms. His vases, for example, such as the one shown above, often have a prickly quality inspired by pineapples, sea urchins, and horsechestnut burrs. He worked in Germany – at the Halier Studio, Frederiksberg, in 1929, and at the Saxbo factory (est. 1929) from 1930. From 1934 he produced designs for the Royal Copenhagen Porcelain factory (est. 1755) in his native Denmark.

* The high-fired stonewares in organic shapes with coloured glazes made at the Halier Studio are keenly collected.
* His pieces often have highly distinctive earth-toned glazes, such as the "Oxblood" glaze shown on the vase above.
* His ceramics are consistently marked with an incised and attenuated Salto name.
* Some pieces made in the early 1930s are also dated.
* Salto's work is particularly popular with American and Scandinavian collectors.

Otto Meier (b.1903)

The German potter Otto Meier initially studied architecture, and his early pieces showed strong sculptural influences Subsequently his open bowls, vases, and vessels had a softer, more organic feel and were decorated with fluxed running glazes. The stoneware "Disc" vessel (c.1950) below is a typical example of his naturalistic forms and fine-quality glazing. From 1978 he began to work with porcelain, producing vessels and wall plaques.
* Meier pieces are marked

with an incised or impressed monogram.

Jan van der Vaart (1931–2000)

The work of the Dutch ceramicist Jan van der Vaart was strongly influenced by the tenets of the De Stijl Movement and the Bauhaus and, characteristically, avoids excessive or ornamental decoration. His plain yet elegant pieces made no attempt to appear handmade: rather they often have architectural mathematical forms constructed from cast elements.
* From 1962 he made a series of Tulip vases, such as the one shown right, designed in 1995, that were based on a traditional form, but made from cast elements.
* The shape of the elements varied, so Tulip vases may have different spouts, etc.
* Tulip vases were made in stoneware and earthenware.
* Many other Vaart pieces are made up of different combinations of the same cast elements.
* Vaart also designed for ceramic manufacturers, including Rosenthal.
* Vaart used a restricted colour palette – blue, white, black, and bronze.
* His one-off studio pieces are rarer and therefore more keenly collected than his designs for commercial manufacturers.

* Vaart's work began to be collected in the 1950s and by the 1960s was bought by major museums.

Other studio potters

Other collectable contemporary European studio ceramicists include the French potter Pierre Bayle (b.1945), and Claudi Casanovas (b.1956) from northern Spain.
* Bayle's ceramics have organic shapes, with characteristic distinctive controlled glazes and remarkable subtle coloured effects.
* Casanovas' large-scale pieces have distinctive forms and surfaces that reflect the influence of the volcanic surroundings of his native Catalunya. They are constructed on a mould, which remains in place as a support while they are fired to high temperatures.

Collecting

* Good condition is essential for all modern ceramics; check for signs of repair or restoration on vulnerable areas.
* Fakes are known, but most contemporary artists have a *catalogue raisonné* that lists their whole body of work.
* Studio ceramics is still a quite small collecting area. Pieces are generally sold through galleries and are correspondingly highly priced. Studio ceramics at auction are also highly priced because of the relatively small output and the high original gallery prices.

ARTIST CERAMICS

Many of the best-known fine artists of the 20thC have used pottery as a medium for expression, usually by experimenting with decorating blanks. The French art dealer Ambrose Vollard (1867–1939) commissioned artists such as Henri Matisse (1869–1954), Georges Rouault (1871–1958), and Pierre Bonnard (1867–1947) to decorate blank vases that he sold through his gallery.

Other artists played a more prominent role in determining shape by collaborating with potters on the forms that they then hand-painted. In Britain, the artist and critic Roger Fry, a self-taught potter, helped design, and sometimes also threw, the pots that were freely hand-painted, by him, Vanessa Bell, and Duncan Grant. In France, Raoul Dufy (1877–1953) collaborated with the Catalan potter Josep Llorens Artigas (1892–1980).

In contrast to those artists who used clay primarily as an alternative to canvas, other painters were commissioned for designs for commercial production runs, adapting their fine-art skills to the constraints of printed tableware patterns, with varying degrees of success. Artists such as Eric Ravilious, and Edward Ardizzone in Britain, and Raymond Peynet in France, who were already familiar with the constraints of book illustration, readily adapted to the new medium, as did Dame Laura Knight, whose fascination with circus life is seen both in her large canvases and the tableware patterns she created for A. J. Wilkinson. The Italian designer Piero Fornasetti used an eclectic range of graphic motifs for his elaborate designs for surface patterns.

In the late 1940s and early '50s Pablo Picasso (1881–1973) produced a prolific range of ceramics that fall into two main categories: ceramic sculptures, in which each piece is unique; and ceramics reproduced in limited editions. He too collaborated on the forms that he hand-painted using motifs – birds, fish, goats, bulls and bull-fighting scenes, and mythological creatures – and a bold, broad brush-stroked painting style familiar from his paintings. Inspired by Picasso, in the 1950s Jean Cocteau (1889–1963) was one of many artists to make small, limited-edition ceramic forms, painting dishes, straight vases, goblets, and plates with playful decoration.

Manufacturers such as Wedgwood often commissioned fine artists to contribute to prestige limited-edition ranges, sometimes following a specific brief. The painter John Piper produced both one-off hand-painted pieces such as plates for the Fulham Pottery, and limited editions of plates for Wedgwood. In about 1970, the Scottish-born sculptor Eduardo Paolozzi (b.1924) created a series of six plates for Wedgwood, who commissioned a limited-edition series of plates with the National Art Collections Fund in 1993 from leading fine artists and sculptors, including Peter Blake, Patrick Caulfield, Patrick Heron, and Bruce McLean.

PIERO FORNASETTI

Pittori Italiani series plate by Piero Fornasetti
1950s; value code H

Identification checklist for Piero Fornasetti ceramics
1. Is it a simple, conservative shape?
2. Does it have transfer-printed decoration?
3. Is the decoration an eclectic mix of graphic motifs, possibly including lettering and gilding?
4. Does it have a surreal quality?
5. Is it marked?

Piero Fornasetti (1913–88)
An engraver, manufacturer, and painter, Fornasetti was also a highly prolific freelance designer of ceramics, producing many witty surface decorations for printed plates and tablewares for a number of manufacturers.

Designs
Fornasetti's innovative designs used an eclectic range of motifs including antique engravings, Renaissance art, architecture, medals, astronomical or ex-catalogue illustrations, hands, faces, and musical instruments.
* Transfer-printed decoration was applied to bone-china blanks – plates, small dishes, cups and saucers, dishes of various sizes and shapes, vases, and cylindrical jars and covers.
* Among his best-known designs

are those for series of plates: the Themes and Variations series used a black-and-white image of a woman's face but added surreal details such as an eye patch; the 12 Mesi, 12 Soli series used the image of a sun with a face to represent the 12 months of the year. One is in black-and-white, the other 11 have polychrome decoration.
* It is often difficult to date pieces accurately with such a prolific designer, but all pieces are clearly marked, usually with both the designer's signature and details of the manufacturer. Marks will vary and are often stylized to reflect the design theme.
* Shapes such as large plates, or large jars and covers, that provide a good surface for complex decoration, are popular, as are limited-edition plates.

35

Tableware by Milner Gray, Dame Laura Knight, and Gordon Forsyth, made for Harrods' Exhibition of 1934; Circus plate; value code H

Identification checklist for Circus Ware by Dame Laura Knight

1. Is it a piece of earthenware tableware, most commonly a plate?
2. Is it decorated with transfer-printed and hand-painted decoration?
3. Does it have a gold-leaf surround?
4. Does the central motif feature one of the acts found in a traditional circus?
5. Is it marked with the artist's name?

Art for the Table

In 1934, the Harrods department store in London, together with E. Brain & Co and A. J. Wilkinson, mounted an Exhibition of Contemporary Art for the Table, which attempted to marry art and industry by commissioning tableware designs from 27 leading contemporary artists.

* Brain & Co. pattern books show 51 designs for the exhibition by various artists.
* Designs emphasized the role of the artist/designer by stamping their names on the bottom and designating the first 12 sets "First Editions".
* Not a commercial success at the time, designs produced by Brain and Wilkinson in bone china and earthenware respectively are keenly collected today.

Dame Laura Knight (1877–1970)

Dame Laura Knight's Circus tableware range was commissioned by Clarice Cliff (see p.122), then art director of A. J. Wilkinson. It was shown in the Harrods' Exhibition and produced in earthenware with a Clarice Cliff Bizarre backstamp that also featured a Laura Knight signature.

* Shapes included teapots, sugar bowls, hot-water jugs, coffee pots with acrobat-shaped handles, and lamp bases.

* Circus pieces are very rare and expensive. Plates like the one in the main picture ranged in diameter from 6 to 18in (15 to 46cm) and are generally the only pieces found.

Edward Ardizzone
(1900–79)

The artist and illustrator Edward Ardizzone's set of Country Pleasures plates were commissioned under the Royal Chelsea label when it was part of Susie Cooper China.
* The charming litho-printed decorations of gently humorous pastoral scenes were based on pen-and-ink drawings by Ardizzone.
* The first six plates – Boating, Drinking, Bathing, Fishing, The Picnic, and Courting, shown below – were produced in 1957 and are now very collectable.

Fulham Pottery

In the early 1980s the Fulham

Pottery commissioned artists to design unusual and decorative ware using traditional materials and production techniques. The Mermaid plate bottom p.36, by Quentin Bell, freely painted in the Bloomsbury style, reflects the influence of his mother, Vanessa Bell, who designed ceramics for the Harrods' Exhibition and the Omega Workshops. The artists Philip Sutton and John Piper (see p.38) also contributed to the series, successfully adapting their painting styles to clay.

Omega Pottery (1913–20)

The painters Roger Fry, Duncan Grant, and Vanessa Bell also designed and decorated ceramics. Poole Pottery offered them facilities for throwing and firing, and from 1914 to 1917 hand-painted pottery from prototypes thrown by Fry were sold through the Omega Workshops.
* Roger Fry became largely responsible for designing shapes.
* Vanessa Bell painted wares with figurative and contemporary scenes and, later, with colourful abstract patterns.
* Grant's hand-painted decoration was typically lively and inventive.

Wedgwood

Wedgwood's tradition of commissioning designs from well-known artists continued in the 20thC with designs by, among others, Eric Ravilious (see p.129), John Skeaping (see pp.90–91) and Eduardo Paolozzi (see p.39).
* Rex Whistler designed the picturesque landscape series Views of Clovelly (c.1932). His brother Laurence Whistler, a glass engraver, designed the Dolphin tableware pattern, and the Outlines of Grandeur series, a set of six plates made in limited editions c.1955.
* In 1977 the watercolourist David Gentleman (b.1930) created a series of views of British castles and country houses. The bone-china plates, with gilded rims, were produced in limited editions of 5,000 and are now collectors' items. The Windsor Castle plate shown below was one of the first two to be issued in 1977.
* In 1993 Wedgwood, in association with the National Art Collections Fund, issued another limited edition of plates commissioned from contemporary

painters and sculptors such as Peter Blake, Patrick Caulfield, Patrick Heron, Bruce McLean, Eduardo Paolozzi, and John Piper.

Collecting
* Any piece carrying the signature of a well-known artist will command a premium, particularly if issued in a limited edition.

ENGLISH II

*Blue Arizona plate by Sir Terry Frost for Poole Pottery
1998; value code H*

Identification checklist for Sir Terry Frost ceramics
1. Is it a large dish plate?
2. Is it decorated by hand?
3. Is it decorated in primary colours?
4. Are the motifs based on circles, half-circles and bands, and other motifs familiar from Frost paintings?
5. Is it signed?

Artist ceramics
Many fine artists simply transferred their characteristic colours, motifs, and painting techniques from canvas to clay; others preferred to adapt to the constraints of the medium, creating patterns that could be applied by hand or by printing to suit different commercial shapes.

Sir Terry Frost (b.1915)
The painter and printmaker Sir Terry Frost, based in Newlyn,

Cornwall, used primary colours and shapes based on circles, half-circles, and bands both in his abstract canvases and in the collectable ceramic designs he produced for Poole Pottery from the late 1990s, such as the Arizona plate shown above, in a characteristic blue.
* Frost created two abstract designs for the standard large Poole dish; they were painted by the Poole paintresses under his supervision.
* The Frost designs were issued in limited editions and carry the Poole mark and a Terry Frost signature.

John Piper (1903–92)
A topographical painter and printmaker, John Piper designed textiles, and, from the 1980s, a large range of moulded ceramics.
* Medium and large platters in

flattened oval shapes decorated with a favourite theme of a bird in flight or abstract designs, some inspired by primitive mythology (see bottom p.38).
* Sets of plates with decorative themes.
* Vases, candlesticks, and curly moulded dishes.

Sir Eduardo Paolozzi (b.1924)

One of Wedgwood's most successful collaborations was with the sculptor Eduardo Paolozzi, who produced complex abstract flat pattern designs for several series of boxed plates issued in limited editions that are now eagerly collected.
* Variations on a Geometric Theme was produced in 1970 and consisted of six silkscreen designs on coupé-shaped bone-china plates. They were issued in a limited edition of 200 sets, each with numbered certificate.
* The plates above are from the Kalkulium Suite, a boxed set of six plates issued in 1987.
* Paolozzi contributed the Fabula plate, with a design of mythological figures in a silver zodiac, to the Wedgwood/National Art Collection Art plates (see p.34). He also created mosaic designs for Tottenham Court Road tube station, in London.

Janice Tchalenko (b.1942)

Tchalenko's ceramics bridge the gap between domestic pottery and the "new ceramics" (see p.28). Her ranges include one-off studio pieces with richly coloured, dramatic decoration combining painted and slip decoration, and commercial ranges for retailers such as Next Interiors, the Dart Pottery (1984), and the London-based Designers' Guild, with decoration after her designs.
* The commercial ranges of domestic ware, such as the pieces below, designed for the Next Interior collection (1985 to 1989) are very affordable.
* The one-off pieces, like large platters with bold, floral decoration and round-bodied jugs with wide flanges, are correspondingly expensive.
* From the late 1990s Tchalenko produced painted wares at Poole Pottery.

Tripod vase by Pablo Picasso
1951; value code B

Identification checklist for Pablo Picasso ceramics
1. Is the piece a conventional form such as a plate?
2. Or is it a highly original, often quirky, form, perhaps constructed from a thrown form with added elements?
3. Does it have freehand painted decoration?
4. Is the decoration boldly executed in bright colours and clearly visible brushwork?
5. Does the decoration transform the shape into a playful representation of an animal or a human form?
6. Is it signed?

Raoul Dufy (1877–1953)
Dufy's collaborative ceramic designs included vases, fountains, and planters.
* The series of over 60 small ceramic gardens painted with flowers, fruit, and figures in characteristically bright yellows and blues.
* Vases were often decorated with images of swans or bathers (see vase, 1935, right), to complement the fluid forms.
* Dufy/Artigas pieces should be individually numbered (1–110).
* Dufy also designed ceramics for the Limoges factory of Haviland et Cie (see p.179).

Pablo Picasso

Picasso was the most prolific and influential artist-potter of the 20thC. From 1947 he worked with Georges and Suzanne Ramie at their Pottery Madoura at Vallauris in the south of France, where he collaborated on designing shapes and adapted thrown shapes by moulding or adding to them (see main picture).

* The most common shapes were round, square, and oblong plates, such as the Visage Noir service below, platters, jugs, and vases. Other more interesting forms were those based on Hellenistic terracotta figurines

of women carrying amphora, the owl shape, and other quirky forms created by adding to a basic thrown shape.

* Favourite motifs include fish, goats, and mythological creatures.
* The one-off ceramic sculptures by Picasso himself are unique and correspondingly highly priced; other ranges of ceramics were produced in limited editions under Picasso's supervision – the vase in the main picture, for example, was issued in a limited edition of 75 – and are less expensive.
* Picasso ceramics have a stamped or incised base mark.

Jean Cocteau (1889–1963)

Inspired by Picasso's ceramics, Cocteau was one of the many artists in the 1950s to make small limited-edition ceramic forms.

* He decorated conventional forms such as plates, dishes, straight vases, and goblets with the playful free-hand linear motifs, such as designs of faces shown in profile, and a favourite faun/satyr motif.
* Cocteau ceramics produced in limited editions have a painted signature and are often marked *Edition originale de Jean Cocteau, Atelier Madeleine-Jolly*, with the limited-edition number.

Raymond Peynet (1908–99)

Peynet's distinctive line illustrations were used on posters, textiles, books, and ceramics. From 1952 he created a highly successful giftware (see lidded dish below, 1960s) range for Rosenthal that included candelabra and novelties.

* Any damage or repairs will greatly reduce value.
* Typically Peynet designs use fine printed linework and pastel colours.
* His work is popular in Japan, where the Yamaka company produced a range of Peynet-decorated ceramics in 1994.

BRITISH CERAMICS

For much of the 20thC the British ceramics industry depended upon its export markets, such as the old colonial markets and the US, and as a result its fortunes were closely linked to the American economy. In the early 20thC companies such as Minton, Royal Crown Derby, and Coalport produced expensive export porcelain, largely in traditional styles and patterns, for the overseas market, especially the US and Australia. Many leading manufacturers subsidized the production of valuable porcelain and decorative wares with the mass-production of everyday, inexpensive domestic wares with hand-painted designs and popular decorative figures. In the 1920s and '30s, manufacturers tried to beat the economic gloom by producing ranges of cheap and cheerful novelties, kitchenware, and tableware which included such now-famous Art Deco and modern designs as Clarice Cliff's Bizarre Ware, expressly designed as inexpensive domestic pottery and launched in 1928.

During WWII, larger firms such as Spode, Wedgwood, and Moorcroft were licensed to manufacture domestic pottery; other firms were forced to close, either permanently or for the duration. These war-time restrictions and post-war austerity meant that in the late 1930s and '40s there was little to buy in Britain other than undecorated Utility ware, as better-quality decorated wares were exported to boost the economy. Post-war top-quality hand-painted decoration was increasingly replaced by mass production, using transfer-printing and litho-printing to reproduce original images, and many established factories no longer used painters.

By the early 1950s, the British ceramics industry was responding to the national drive for exports and the need to earn foreign currency. The Festival of Britain in 1951 showcased British design talent, and companies such as Midwinter were producing mid-quality brightly coloured and decorated modern household wares, for which there was a large market as people rebuilt and refurnished their homes in the new American-inspired freeform styles.

The traditional export markets helped British manufacturers to flourish, and in the 1960s, British fashion and design was at the forefront of world style. From the 1970s onwards, however, British manufacturers were adversely affected by the oil crisis, increased competition from Chinese and Japanese manufacturers, and numerous mergers, and the British ceramics industry was increasingly run by organizations that knew little about making pottery. By the 1970s Wedgwood, Royal Doulton, and Royal Worcester Spode dominated production. These groupings have since changed again, and the large conglomerates are now facing competition from smaller, dynamic companies whose products can adjust more quickly to the demands of a volatile fashion-conscious market.

JAMES SADLER & SONS

Racing Car teapot by James Sadler & Sons 1940s; value code H

Identification checklist for teapots by James Sadler & Sons
1. Is the piece a teapot, often in an unusual shape?
2. Is it a moulded shape?
3. Is it made of earthenware?
4. Is it brightly coloured?
5. Does it have a printed or impressed mark?

James Sadler & Sons
Founded in 1882 in Burslem, Staffordshire, by the 1930s the firm was producing a huge range of wares in the contemporary style, including artware, but Sadler's best-known wares are probably teapots.

Teapots
Among the most sought-after of Sadler's teapots are the novelty pieces made for the popular end of the market from the 1930s and throughout the 1950s.
* 1920s: Handy Hexagonal

spoutless teapot in various colours and six different sizes.
* 1930s: a range of new teapot patterns, plain and hand-decorated, matt glazes; and Modernist patterns and shapes.

* The racing-car teapot manufactured in 1938 was produced in blue with silver lustre, and in pink and yellow. It often appeared with the registration number OKT 42.
* Other 1930s novelty designs included a Father Christmas teapot; a tank-shaped teapot with a lid featuring a Winston Churchill-like head wearing a tin helmet; a Bunny teapot, with a lid formed by the ears; a Football teapot; and a Crinoline Lady teapot marked "Ye daintee laydee".
* 1950s designs include teapots featuring chocolate-box style illustrations of country cottages and crinolined ladies with moulded gilt frames and lid knobs shaped as gilded bows.
* 1960s: coffee pots in tall-sided cylindrical shapes with stylized floral patterns.
* The Heirloom Collection of reproduction teapots featured archive designs. The teapot left, for example, is a 1930s design reproduced in the 1990s.
* Other ornamental teapot ranges included English Country Cottages, Camelot Castles, and the London Heritage Collection.

43

*Art Deco wall mask by Beswick
1930s; value code H*

Identification checklist for Beswick wall masks
1. Is the piece modelled in low relief?
2. Does it have a model number on the back?
3. If made pre-WWII does it have a high gloss glaze?
4. If made post-war, does it have a matt glaze?
5. Does it have an Art Deco look?
6. Does it reflect contemporary films and fashions?

Beswick (est. 1894)
When John Beswick took over the family firm in Longton, Staffordshire, in 1921, he phased out the 19thC traditions of his father and introduced many lines that reflected contemporary taste. He had a real talent for spotting and anticipating new trends and employed a series of talented designers, establishing Beswick as a remarkably diverse pottery that made a huge range of domestic and decorative goods, many of which are highly sought after because they epitomize the fashion of the day.

"Popular" Modernism
In the 1930s, Beswick introduced a range of domestic earthenwares in modern shapes, some with matt glazes, that can be loosely classified as "popular" Modernism. They included:
* naturalistic embossed moulded salad wares;
* tableware, including the highly

popular Sundial range, such as the teapot and butter dish shown right, with its mark that reflected the stamp of Royal approval;

* moulded hand-painted Art Deco vases and jugs – now keenly collected;
* fruit ware, such as the orange marmalade pot bottom p.44, that was made into the 1950s.

Animal models
John Beswick built on the company's 19thC tradition of

well-modelled flat-backed animal figures by launching, in 1938, the first naturalistically modelled horse, Bois Russell, designed by sculptor Arthur Gedington.
* Gedington also modelled foals, farm and wild animals, dogs, birds, and figures.
* By the mid-1940s model animals were one of the company's mainstays.
* By the 1950s Beswick employed a number of highly skilled modellers for its range of authentically modelled horses. The typically diverse collection shown above was made in the 1950s and '60s.
* Among the most collectable models are the rearing

Lippizaner Stallion, the figure from the Spanish Riding School, Vienna, and the Dulux Dog, now an advertising icon, which was produced as promotional material for the paint manufacturers in the 1960s (see p.117).

Face masks
Perhaps inspired by imported wooden African masks, ceramic wall masks in bold colours and with sharp contours became very popular in the 1930s. Austrian manufacturers such as Goebel, Royal Dux, and, in particular, Goldscheider (see p.174), made striking top-quality, well-modelled masks that are now very collectable. Beswick was one of the leading British manufacturers and produced a range of wall masks of famous film stars and fashionable young women, both in profile, and face on.
* One of his most popular ranges was based on Marlene Dietrich – both face on, in profile (rarer), and in numerous colourways. The red-headed version is rare and collectable.
* Among the other leading British manufacturers was the Staffordshire company of J. H. Cope & Co Ltd.
* Clarice Cliff also designed a range of face masks (see p.123).
* Masks by the same manufacturer will be similar in style and finish and are often collected and displayed in groups.

"SUNDIAL"
AS PURCHASED
BY
H.M. QUEEN MARY.

BESWICK II

*Zebra-striped vases by Beswick
mid-1950s; value code I*

Identification checklist for Beswick Zebra-striped Ware
1. Does the piece have bold black-and-white stripes on the outside?
2. Does it have a bright yellow or red interior?
3. Does it have a daring asymmetrical and organic shape?
4. Is the shape contemporary and sculptural?
5. Is it typically 1950s in style?
6. Does it have a simple backstamp marked "BESWICK ENGLAND REGISTRATION APPLIED FOR"?

1950s domestic wares
Beswick's reputation as a trend-setter was made with a range of highly popular, and now very collectable domestic wares, transfer-printed with quint-essentially 1950s patterns that

included:
* Mexican Madness, with sombreros and cacti, which captured the contemporary enthusiasm for foreign travel;
* Ballet (also referred to as

Pavlova on its backstamp), showing groups and pairs of ballet dancers, which was one of the most popular 1950s designs and is readily found as it was produced in large quantities;
* Circus, seen on the "telly set" cup and plate left, which is one of the most popular collecting niches, with coffee and teapots, in particular, commanding a premium.

Nursery ware characters
The Beatrix Potter characters shown at the top of p.47, were produced from c.1947 under licence from Frederick Warne, the original publishers of the books. They are one of the most popular Beswick collecting ranges. By 1966 there were more than 30 Beatrix Potter characters. Some of the other collectable lines include:
* characters from Alice in Wonderland;

Berry, Freesia, Anemone, fish, Orchid, and Hazeldene.
* The flambé glazed pieces are among Moorcroft's most outstanding wares.

Patterns

Landscape designs featuring sinuous trees and hills were very popular then and now, and used on Florian Ware and many other shapes in the 1920s and '30s.
* The later landscape designs of 1920s include Moonlit Blue (1922), Eventide (1923) with rich oranges, reds, and greens, and Dawn (1926) (below left) in pale blue, white, and yellow with a matt finish.
* Pomegranate (introduced 1911) was one of Moorcroft's most successful patterns, with subtle colours blending over slip

W. MOORCROFT des; or WM des; many pieces are marked FLORIAN WARE JAS. MACINTYRE & CO. LTD BURSLEM ENGLAND.
* Late Florian Ware (1918–23), also featured tightly drawn flowers and flowing forms but in stronger, richer colours, such as blue, green, and yellow.

Flambé wares

Moorcroft produced his first rouge flambé glazes by 1922 and became a master of the process, making flambé wares until 1945.
* The copper-based flambé glazes included rich reds, yellows, and browns shot through with other colours.
* They were used both for plain flambé wares, as an overlay on decorative wares (see the vase right with the popular leaf-and-grape pattern, c.1935), and for the wares mounted in decorative silver, electroplate pewter, and brass mounts.
* Other popular designs used with flambé include Leaf and

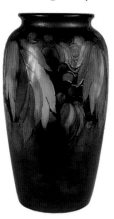

trailing and pale or mottled grounds (green or yellow until 1914; deep blues and purples from 1916).
* Pansy, seen on the vase above left, designed by James Macintyre was introduced in 1910 on white, ivory, or celadon grounds; dark blue was used from 1916.
* The toadstool pattern, known as Claremont by Liberty's, was introduced in 1903 and made for nearly 40 years.
* The Persian range (1914–20), was a new pattern and featured intertwined flowers in strong colours on pale grounds.
* The Blue Porcelain range (1913–63) of speckled blue tableware was sold through Liberty's as Powder Blue.

MOORCROFT II

Bermuda Lily range by Walter Moorcroft
c.1970; value codes G/H

Identification checklist for Walter Moorcroft ceramics
1. Is it hand-thrown or slip-cast?
2. Are the patterns applied to a series of
related shapes?
3. Are the ground colours pale?
4. Is the decoration based on identifiable flowers?
5. Is the decoration tube-lined and hand-painted?
6. Is it signed WM?

Walter Moorcroft
(1917–2002)

The economic slump in the 1930s forced William Moorcroft to reintroduce the use of pale grounds and intensive application of matt glazes and withdrew several earlier styles. His son Walter joined the firm briefly in 1935, and took over in 1945, following his father's sudden death. As skilled a designer as his father, Walter maintained Moorcroft's reputation for decorative hand-made pottery and introduced his own range of patterns from 1947.

Patterns

Most of Walter Moorcroft's patterns were inspired by indigenous and foreign flowers. Early floral patterns such as Columbine and Clematis (1947) showed William's influence, but from the 1950s Walter showed a preference for more exotic patterns in dramatic colours.
* Floral patterns include Hibiscus, Bougainvillea, African Lily, Arum Lily, Campanula, Wild Arum, and Tulip.
* Many patterns were produced

in a variety of colourways. The Bermuda Lily pattern was initially designed with a turquoise ground; it was also made with white flowers on olive green, yellow flowers on ivory, and yellow flowers on brown (shown above).
* Less typical are, Caribbean (1961–c.1963), with brightly coloured beaches, palm trees, and boats, designed for a range of tankards, vases, and trays for a company in Bermuda; and Marine (1962–64), another brightly coloured pattern featuring sea horses, fish, and seaweed.
* Leaves in the Wind was also untypical and produced only from 1960 to 1962.
* Walter developed a new version of the popular Anemone pattern in 1975 and in 1989.

Modern wares

From the late 1980s until 1992, Sally Tuffin became principal designer, launching a series of new patterns including:
* bird-and-fruit themes;
* fruit – Plum, Lemon (both 1988–90);

* fish (see vase 1980s , below).
* Tulips, introduced 1989, based on a William Morris fabric;
* peacock feathers, originally a Liberty & Co. exclusive;
* special and limited-edition designs featuring balloons, penguins, ships, owls, cats, and elephants such as the tube-lined polar bear vase of 1988, made in a limited edition of 250 for the Canadian market.
* Rachel Bishop and other designers have continued the Moorcroft tradition to the present day.

Marks

The Moorcroft factory used various marks, including:
* paper labels with printed factory mark;
* Moorcroft signature or initials, painted or incised retailer's mark;
* design registration number and pattern or shape mark;
* MOORCROFT BURSLEM, impressed with either WM or W. MOORCROFT;
* some important pieces have dates;
* Potter to the Queen mark used from 1929.

Influence

William Moorcroft was one of the most successful English ceramicists in the Art Nouveau

style, introducing and popularizing organic, swirling naturalistic decoration based on recognizable flora and fauna. His use of flowing slip-trailed designs was copied by many other manufacturers, including Hancock & Sons, who were best known for their Morris Ware, which featured elaborately coloured tube-lined decoration as seen on the vase above of c.1910.

Collecting

In general, early Moorcroft is most eagerly collected, with patterns and glazes rather than forms determining appeal.
* Florian Ware remains among the finest examples of English Art Nouveau.
* Hazeldene, produced from 1902, is particularly popular, especially the large dramatic flambé vases of the 1930s.
* Other popular patterns are Eventide, Moonlit Blue and Dawn – all 1920s landscapes –, especially when combined with rich flambé glaze; and Claremont and Pomegranate.
* Pieces signed by William Moorcroft are especially collectable but expensive; those signed by Walter are generally more affordable.
* The special limited editions produced by Sally Tuffin are now very sought after.
* Moorcroft wares are often damaged as the body is quite soft. Some restoration is acceptable, if well done, but condition affects value.
* Powder Blue tableware (1913–63) has impressed marks but is never signed.
* Good-quality fakes, notably Florian patterns, are now being made in China, complete with signatures and marks.

BURGESS & LEIGH

Golf jug by Burgess & Leigh
c.1930s; value code F

Identification checklist for Burleigh Ware Sporting jugs
1. Is it made of earthenware?
2. Is it an eccentric shape?
3. Is it hand-painted?
4. Does it depict a sporting activity – tennis, golf, cricket – that was popular in the 1930s?
5. Does it have black painted dots on the rim?
6. Does it have a Burleigh Ware mark on the base?

Burgess & Leigh
Established in 1862 in Burslem, Staffordshire, from 1877 the company traded as Burgess & Leigh, making a range of underglaze decorated earthenware tablewares,

kitchenwares, and dinnerware in traditional styles. By the 1920s the company was producing tableware patterns en suite to coordinate with tea, fruit, and salad sets. From the 1930s, production was marked Burleigh Ware (see right).

Jugs
In the 1930s the company launched a range of hand-painted jugs that were hugely popular at the time and are eagerly collected today.
* Examples in typically Art Deco colours such as yellow are more collectable than those in more muted tones.
* The Animal jugs feature a range of different animals – flamingos, kingfishers, parrots,

squirrels, rabbits (on Harvest jugs) monkeys, and dragons – that either form the handle of the jug (more collectable) or decorate the body. Among the rarest are the jugs with sloth handles.
* The Parrot jugs, seen here, made c.1930s, are especially

popular and form a separate collecting niche as no two are the same.
* Sporting jugs are another collecting niche. Again, no two are the same, and in general, those with more individual detail – such as the checked trousers shown on the Golf jug in the main picture, rather than plain trousers seen on other versions – are more popular.

Charlotte Rhead
A major coup, announced in press advertisements, was the arrival of the distinguished designer Charlotte Rhead (see p.127), who worked for Burgess & Leigh from 1926 to 1931 and produced many new patterns for ornamental and functional wares.
* Early Rhead designs appear under the Burleigh mark and were applied to shapes already in production.
* Later Rhead designed both new shapes and patterns.
* Designs include fruit-and-

flower patterns, and abstract and geometric designs such as Florentine, Sylvan, and Garland, with black tube-lining on white grounds with blue-and-gold patterns.
* Wares marked with Charlotte Rhead's signature are eagerly collected.

Later domestic wares
After post-war restrictions were lifted, Burgess & Leigh re-launched their domestic wares in the 1950s with the Fantasia range – a stylish interpretation of the new contemporary look – as seen on the sideplate shown on p.54, made in 1959.
* Fantasia reflected the 1950s fascination with graphic decoration featuring contemporary domestic items, as seen also on the Homemaker range produced by Ridgway (see p.100).
* Designed by Harold Bennett, it was produced in fashionable black-and-white.
* Manchester City Museum and Art Gallery commissioned a reproduction issue of Fantasia for commercial sale in the 1990s. These later pieces have a modern backstamp to distinguish them from early originals.

In the 1990s, the company gave traditional domestic ware forms a new look using a fresh interpretation of the traditional blue-and-white and all-over chintzware patterns on the Calico kitchenware range, and the newly fashionable, revived traditional decorative techniques of stencilling and sponging on tea and coffee wares.

CARLTON WARE I

*Chinoiserie vase by Carlton Ware
c.1920s; value code G*

Identification checklist for Carlton Ware lustre ware
1. Does it have an iridescent, high-gloss glaze?
2. Does it have good-quality hand-painted enamelling and freehand gilding on glaze?
3. Does it have an Oriental-inspired shape?
4. Does it have exotic Oriental-inspired decoration?
5. Does it have a richly coloured jewel-like appearance?
6. Does it have a Carlton Ware mark (see right)?

Carlton Ware
Carlton Ware was the trademark used from the mid-1890s by the firm of Wiltshaw & Robinson, established in 1890 in Stoke-on-Trent, Staffordshire. From 1920, the firm gained a reputation for decorative ceramics in Oriental-inspired shapes, glazes, and patterns, with lustre and lacquer effects, such as the Chinoiserie vase shown above.

The three major types of Carlton Wares in the 1920s and 1930s were exotically coloured lustre art pottery; geometric design work; and moulded earthenware teaware and salad ware decorated with fruit and flowers, and small novelty wares (see p.58).

Lustre wares
Carlton's lustre ware was produced in the wake of Wedgwood's successful Fairyland lustre range (see p.10 and p.88). The technique involved the controlled use of an iridescent, high-gloss, pearlized glaze, which gave pieces a richly coloured, jewel-like appearance. Any irregularities caused by the firing were concealed by the gilt detail applied freehand afterwards.
* Individual designers are not identified.
* Ground colours included powder-blue and rose du Barry.
* The 12 lustre colours included mother-of-pearl, orange, red, turquoise, and black.

* A cobalt blue ground, seen in the main picture, was commonly used.

Royale wares

One of the most popular ranges in the 1920s, Royale lustre wares included vases, jugs, dishes, trays, plates, and ginger jars and came in a variety of colours.
* Rouge (red) Royale, as seen in the jug above made in 1925, together with green, are very popular colours.
* Popular patterns include the Humming Bird design shown above, which is also known as Bird in Flight.

Handcraft range

The Handcraft range was made for a limited period only and is rare and highly sought after.
* Most Handcraft pieces were vases decorated with exotic patterns in enamels and gilding.
* Pieces with geometric patterns made in the 1920s and '30s are very rare and sought after.
* Handcraft has its own backstamp – a script mark in blue, together with an impressed shape number, a painted pattern number and, in some cases, a gilder's mark.
* Handcraft pieces were made with matt and high-gloss glazes.

Decoration

The success of Carlton Ware was due largely to the superb quality of the hand-painted decoration, gilding, glaze effects, and the variety of the patterns.
* The Sunflower pattern, used on a variety of shapes including jugs, dishes, and vases, had an unusual hand-painted ground.
* Large Sunflower pieces are most collectable but rare.
* The pattern appears both with the butterfly, as seen on the vase right, whose large size and gilded rim make it very collectable,

and without; pieces with the butterfly are more collectable.

Collecting

Prices for Carlton's lustre range have increased dramatically in recent years, although they are still lower than those for the lustre wares of their closest rival, Wedgwood.
* Large lustre-ware pieces, such as vases and ginger jars, which offer a generous surface for painted decoration, are most sought after.
* Chinoiserie-style lustre ware is more popular than pieces decorated with fairy gardens and magical landscapes.
* Pieces with geometric decoration and a matt or semi-matt glaze are very rare and therefore eagerly collected.
* Professional re-gilding is expensive but may be worthwhile with large, valuable pieces. Avoid poorly restored examples, where the new gilding (often gold paint and glaze) does not match the original.

CARLTON WARE II

*Apple Blossom cheese dish and vase by Carlton Ware, 1930s;
value code I each*

Identification checklist for Carlton Ware moulded tableware
1. Is it made of earthenware?
2. Does it have moulded textured and embossed decoration?
3. Is the decoration based on fruit and flowers?
4. Is it hand-painted?
5. Is the background colour yellow or green?
6. Does it have a Carlton Ware script mark?

Moulded earthenware tableware

In the 1930s Carlton Ware launched a range of cheap and cheerful moulded earthenware in novel designs, bright colours, and textured fruit and floral patterns to lift the atmosphere of economic gloom. From c.1930 much of the embossed tableware was marked with the script mark shown right. Some pieces also had an impressed number.
* The Apple Blossom pattern seen in the main picture and the moulded dish (1930s) below was

applied to many shapes including mugs, teapots, cups,

and bowls. It was produced in large quantities from c.1936 to 1940 in two colour schemes: yellow and pale green.
* The Cherries pattern is rare and therefore more collectable.
* The strong green and chrome-yellow base colours of the Fruit Basket pattern make it popular with collectors today.
* The Foxglove range included a beaker with a lid that doubled up as a saucer. Lids are rarely found and add to value.
* The Redcurrant and Blackcurrant patterns are distinguished only by the base

colour: yellow for the former and green for the latter.

Later tableware
During the 1950s Carlton Ware

was produced in softer shapes and more muted colours, a trend that continued into the 1960s. The Windswept Ware shown in the advertisement above, with its fluid lines, integral handles, and simple transfer-printed decoration, is a good example of "organic Modernism" in 1950s British tableware.
* Windswept was made in fashionable organic Modernist shapes.
* The two-tone colour combinations include matt brown and cream, glossy pale blue and bottle green, and dusky pink and pale blue.

In the 1970s Carlton introduced the Wellington coffee set, with its distinctive tall cylinder shape with an undulating outline, and, from 1973, Walking Ware, a range of tableware supported on short legs that ended in feet clad in bright socks and shoes (see p.14).

Collecting tableware
* 1930s moulded tableware was produced in large quantities for everyday use so it is readily found but must be in perfect condition to attract collectors.
* Although a design classic, the Windswept range is often less popular with collectors who prefer the more brightly coloured and decorated wares.
* The "Hazlenut" pattern 1950s teapots in both light/dark green

and brown-and-cream colourways are keenly collected.
* The quirky Walking Ware is eagerly collected but often difficult to find as few pieces have survived with the feet undamaged.
* Condition is paramount. A low price may reflect poor restoration, so check pieces carefully, especially vulnerable items such as toast racks or ceramic salad servers.

Advertising and novelty wares
Novelties have been part of the Carlton Ware range from the 1920s. Although traditionally often a good starting-point for collectors, rarer novelties, such as the Carlton Ware hand-bell set of the 1930s, are now commanding higher prices, and the 1960s advertising wares for drinks companies are now so keenly collected that fakes are being made.
* Best-known are the Guinness-related items, in particular those with the Toucan motif, especially the freestanding Toucan (see p.116).
* Other witty 1960s designs

include Beefeater salt and pepper sets and novelty money boxes.
* From the 1970s Carlton Ware produced novelty teapots, such as the popular Red Baron teapot of the 1990s.
* The quirky red shoe bookends above, made in the 1970s, appear in the company's shop book. They may have been inspired by a trip to the Biba department store in London.

Fakes
Fake novelty and advertising wares have been made using moulds that went missing when the factory premises were sold in 1989.

CROWN DEVON

*Orient vase by Crown Devon
late 1920s; value code H*

Identification checklist for Crown Devon Orient Ware
1. Is the decoration hand-painted?
2. Is the design based on geometric motifs?
3. Is the colour scheme vibrant: black, green, red, and yellow, or red, black, and white?
4. Is it an innovative Art Deco shape?
5. Is the piece marked?

Crown Devon
Crown Devon was the trade name used by S. Fielding & Co., established in Stoke-on-Trent, Staffordshire, in 1870. Pattern books for the early 1920s included fine Art Deco tea and coffee services and table accessories. By the mid-1920s the Crown Devon range included inexpensive moulded earthenware novelties, as well as vases, dishes, wall plaques, and figures, and, from the mid-1930s, a range of giftware and tableware. Wares are marked Crown Devon (see right), and some designs feature the artist's mark.

Collectable Art Deco wares
Wares in innovative shapes and vibrant Art Deco colour schemes attract the most interest. The Orient pattern shown in the main picture, used also on coffee sets, lamp-bases, ginger jars, and pen holders, is one of Crown

Devon's finest. Other collecting niches include:
* Moulded earthenware tablewares with embossed floral

patterns such as Belle Fleur with modelled poppies, pansies, and other flowers. Top condition is essential.

* Jugs decorated with Cubist or other Modernist-influenced patterns in bright colours.
* New shapes such as the octagonal Era tableware.
* Novelties such as moulded salad ware in the form of Savoy cabbage leaves, beehive-shaped honey pots, orange-shaped marmalade pots, and tomato trays with high-relief moulded tomatoes.
* Vases, dishes, and wall plaques in innovative shapes and vibrant colour schemes.

Vases were stock-in-trade for all major manufacturers, and the shape of the vase shown at the bottom of p.60 was very popular in the 1930s, having a good surface for showing off hand-painted decoration. This example has a matt ground and on-glaze hand-painted decoration, which makes it particularly desirable. It may be a sample as tube-lined decoration is extremely rare on Crown Devon pieces. The pattern, which combines floral decoration with a spider's web – both motifs commonly found separately – is also unusual. Several leading companies such as Wilton and Carlton Ware produced similar but more expensive versions of this type of hand-painted vase.

Decoration and forms

Crown Devon wares reflected contemporary trends in ceramics, sometimes based on successful lines by other companies.
* The 1950s hors d'oeuvre dish below was inspired by a Poole Pottery precedent. Its organic shape, soft colour, and stylish graphic marine decoration are quintessential features of '50s design.
* 1960s wares included straight-sided cylinder-shaped ceramic storage jars with lower-case lettering and stylized Mary Quant-inspired daisy motifs in red, orange, and black (see p.113), and white Op Art decorated wares.
* A range of novelty teapots was introduced in the 1970s.

Memphis Ware

The classic Egyptian-inspired Memphis range was designed for Crown Devon in the 1960s by Colin Melbourne (see p.47) and is one of his most recognized ranges.
* Memphis vases were made in a variety of shapes from simple to elegant.
* The bright gold chevrons were combined with black, white, and pink (seen below) or the rarer turquoise-coloured glaze.
* Memphis Ware has its own Crown Devon mark that includes Melbourne's script signature.

POOLE POTTERY I

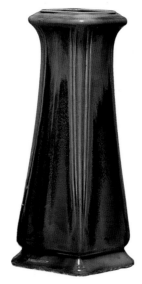

Lustre vase by Poole Pottery
c.1906; value code H

Identification checklist for Poole Pottery lustre wares
1. Does it have an Art Nouveau-inspired form?
2. Is it hand-thrown?
3. Does it have a lustre glaze, usually in red or green?
4. Is the colour irregular?
5. Does it have an impressed Carter & Co script mark?

Poole Pottery
Originally established in Poole, Dorset, in 1873, by 1901 the company was trading as Carter & Co. and added the first Poole art pottery, in the form of lustre-glazed vases, such as the one in the main picture, candlesticks, dishes and jardinières, to its existing range. After WWI, the firm expanded production to meet the demand for decorative pottery, and from 1921, now trading as Carter, Stabler & Adams, a series of talented designers and decorators developed a range of decorative wares in a modern style that used traditional handcraft techniques. These distinctive hand-thrown wares decorated with hand-painted floral and geometric patterns under a matt glaze established the Poole reputation and are keenly collected. The covered jar shown on p.62 was made c.1922, and with its sprigged floral designs hand-painted onto a rich opaque glaze is typical of Carter, Stabler and Adams' first wares.

John and Truda Adams
This husband-and-wife team were instrumental in Poole's success in the 1920s and 1930s. John Adams designed some of the 1920s shapes and glazes, and Truda Adams (Truda Carter from 1931) created the patterns. Another important partnership was that of Harold and Phoebe Stabler, who respectively designed shapes and modelled figures.

* Picotee Ware, also introduced in 1932, had a magnolia body decorated with sprayed bands in a range of subtle colours applied using the aerograph technique.

Collecting 1920s and 1930s wares
* Less densely patterned pieces that pre-date the floral patterns are often more modestly priced.
* The small coffee and tea sets with sparse decoration are now keenly collected and sets can be built up over time.
* Figurative patterns, such as that on the "Leipzig Girl" charger (1926) below left, are unusual. An early date makes this a highly collectable piece.
* Large ornamental wares with an all-over hand-painted pattern in the typical Poole palette are very popular. Condition should be perfect and the decoration should have crisp, clear outlines, and sharp definition.
* There are many Poole collectors' clubs.

* Typically, Poole patterns are based on floral or bird motifs, usually in harmonious blends of deep subtle colours, especially blue.
* The stylized floral designs of the 1930s are very popular, in particular, floral patterns in pastel colours on a matt ground.
* Early dramatic abstract patterns by Truda Adams (see p.126) are fine examples of English Jazz Age Modernism.
* Among the best-known patterns are Bluebird, which was produced in two versions: an early one

Marks
* Most wares are marked on the

with a bird in flight and a later one with the bird sitting on a twig; and the Persian Deer pattern seen on the vase (1930s) right, which typically combines a stylized floral pattern and a matt ivory ground.

Poole Modernism
In the early 1930s Poole introduced several new ranges influenced by the Modernist style.
* The Everest range of ridged and banded wares was produced in a semi-matt finish in white and pastel shades and was similar in style to Keith Murray's range for Wedgwood (see p.121).

base: Carter, Stabler, Adams Ltd or POOLE ENGLAND.
* Virtually all Poole pieces are marked; few are dated.
* Most of the many artists who worked for Poole marked their designs with a decorator's monogram.
* Many pieces have pattern codes – usually consisting of two letters. If a third letter is included, it generally indicates the main colour.

POOLE POTTERY II

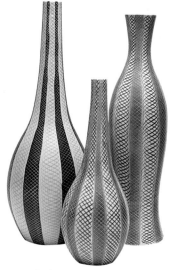

Freeform vases by Poole Pottery mid-1950s; value code H each

Identification checklist for Poole Pottery Freeform vases
1. Is the piece slip-cast or thrown?
2. Is it a flowing organic shape?
3. Is the decoration hand-painted?
4. Is the abstract, complex, and graphic decoration inspired by textile designs?
5. Does the decoration complement the form?
6. Is it marked?

Design classics
Each decade Poole produced classic designs with either hand-thrown, slip-cast, and moulded bodies that made full use of its talented team of decorators, whose monogram was included on the mark.

Streamline
In 1936 John Adams designed the Streamline tableware range, whose fluid machine-made shape exemplifies Poole's Modernist approach in the 1930s.
* Streamline became the first standard competitive Poole tableware and anticipated the

designs of Poole's 1950s and '60s tableware.

* It was made in various patterns: one designed by Truda Carter; simplified designs by Ruth Pavely; or the two-tone finish with soft vellum glazes shown in the coffee set of c.1938, elements seen bottom p.64.

Freeform

Design director Alfred Burgess Read and chief thrower Guy Sydenham created Freeform in the 1950s.

* The dramatic designs reflected the contemporary enthusiasm for Scandinavian style and textiles with abstract decoration (see p.172).

* The complexity of the hand-painted pattern determines price and collectability; simpler patterns and shapes are more modestly priced.

* Freeform vases, either slip-cast or hand-thrown, are now among the most expensive of all Poole pieces.

* The new limited-edition Freeform pieces produced for Liberty's, London, can be identified by their less complex patterns.

Delphis

The huge and varied Delphis decorative ware range was developed from the Poole Studio range by Robert Jefferson, resident designer from 1958, Guy Sydenham, and the designer Tony Morris, in collaboration with the highly skilled Poole paintresses.

* Delphis, launched at Heal's, London, in 1963 and produced until 1980, bridged the gap between commercial and

studio pottery.

* Its strong shapes and exuberant vibrant colourways are typical of the 1960s.

* The dramatic, largely abstract, designs on the late 1960s vases above were created individually by the Poole paintresses.

* Glaze colours were rationalized c.1977 and matt and semi-matt finishes replaced by a glossy glaze.

* Many pieces are marked with the decorator's signature or monogram and a distinguished name will influence value.

Later Poole

Hand-painted ware remained the mainstay throughout various takeovers, including that of 1963

when the company was renamed Poole Pottery. In the 1990s, Sally Tuffin joined the list of distinguished Poole designers and created a number of art ranges, including the Parasol dish, c.1996 above.

Marks

* Dolphin symbol, with Poole, England, used from the 1960s.

65

SHELLEY

A selection of tea and coffee wares by Shelley
c.1930; value codes H/I

Identification checklist for Shelley tea and coffee wares
1. Are the wares slip-cast?
2. Are they made in good-quality translucent bone china?
3. Are they in distinctive, innovative forms, with unusual shaped handles?
4. Are they signed?
5. Do the rims have silver lustre or coloured banding?
6. Is the decoration hand-painted or transfer-printed?
7. Are the patterns Art Deco or Modernist?

Shelley
The company, originally known as Wileman & Co., later traded under Foley, changing its name to Shelley's in 1925 and Shelley Potteries in 1928. In 1919, Eric Slater joined the firm, introducing an aggressive marketing policy and an innovative range of Art Deco designs that were among the finest British inter-war bone-china teawares.

Tea and coffee wares
In the 1920s and '30s Slater designed a range of innovative Art Deco shapes and patterns that, although often highly impractical, are now keenly collected.
* Mode (as shown in the trio top left, p.67) and Vogue (main picture, bottom left) had solid triangular handles and conical-shaped cups.

* Due to the impractical handles they were difficult to use and had a limited production period (1930–31 for Mode, 1930–33 for Vogue), which makes them rarer today.
* Eve had conical cups but a

modified open triangular handle and square plates. The more practical shape ensured longer production (c.1932–38) so it is more readily found.
* The Queen Anne design (main picture) had delicate octagonal hollow ware and square plates. It was registered in 1926 and issued with over 170 patterns.
* Regent (1932–39), with a practical round handle, was one of the best-selling shapes and is readily found.

Patterns

The tea and coffee wares were decorated with a variety of patterns, hand-painted, transfer-printed, and sometimes a combination of the two.
* Early hand-painted patterns included traditional floral and garden scenes.
* Among the most commonly found patterns are Sunrise and Tall Trees, and the hand-painted and transfer-printed Peaches and Grapes pattern shown on the coffee pot (main picture).
* Contemporary Art Deco patterns of powerful abstract designs, such as Sunray, in striking colour combinations such as red and black (see the Mode teaware trio above), red, black and brown, yellow and black, or green and gold, are most popular with collectors.
* The rare hand-painted modern floral designs that exploit the quality of the china ground are also keenly collected.

Nursery wares

Shelley's nursery ware range was first introduced in 1902. It became increasingly successful in the 1920s with a new range of designs by Mabel Lucie Attwell and Hilda Cowham.
* Designs in novelty shapes included toadstool-shaped teapots.
* The Attwell nursery ware

range included cups and saucers, mugs, plates, teapots, napkin rings, and chamber pots.
* Wares were decorated with characters from Attwell's stories, including the popular Boo Boos.
* The range of figures and groups inspired by Attwell's drawings, such as the Our Pets group (1920s) shown below, are rare and very collectable.
* Cowham produced a Children at Play series, registered in 1924.

Harmony Art Ware

Eric Slater also supervised the development of the Harmony Art Ware range, introduced in 1932.
* The wares had hard earthenware bodies.
* The decoration consisted of

coloured glazes poured, dripped, or brushed on to the shape as it turned on the wheel, producing bands of running colours.
* This decoration was used on bone-china teasets and other tableware.
* Harmony was produced in a variety of colour combinations: pink and grey are the rarest.
* The ginger jar on p.66 was a very popular shape in the 1930s with a good surface for decoration.

SYLVAC

*Novelty rabbit by SylvaC
1930s; value code H*

Identification checklist for SylvaC novelty animals
1. Is the form that of a character dog, cat, lamb, frog, hare, or rabbit?
2. Are identical models made in different sizes?
3. Is the animal part of a jug, wall pocket, or other domestic ware?
4. Is it moulded earthenware?
5. Is the glaze a muted colour, such as beige, grey, blue, green, brown, or soft pink?
6. Is it marked?

SylvaC
Trading as Shaw & Copestake in Stoke-on-Trent, Staffordshire, in 1901, the name SylvaC was first used in the mid-1930s, when SylvaC was producing tableware as well as the animal figures and a range of moulded and matt-glazed earthenware ornaments for which it is best known.

Collecting
The animal range, introduced in the late 1920s, is increasing in value.
* Dogs and rabbits are very popular. The dog range includes a number of breeds.
* Similar animal and bird models were made by rival factories. These should always be less valuable.

* Jugs with moulded handles in the form of animals are keenly collected, but simpler jugs and 19thC designs are cheaper.
* Art Deco ornaments such as wall pockets, posy vases, and bookends are sought after.
* Pieces with detailed moulding and naturalistic modelling are more collectable than those with more dramatic shapes, such as this 1930s vase.

E. RADFORD

Art Deco landscape vase by E. Radford
c.1930; value code H

Identification checklist for Art Deco artware by E. Radford
1. Is the piece made of earthenware?
2. Does it have freehand hand-painted decoration?
3. Is the pattern floral or foliate and in soft colours?
4. Does it have a stippled background?
5. Does it have a facsimile script E. Radford mark?

E. Radford
By the 1920s Edward Thomas Brown Radford had set up an independent Radford Handcraft

Pottery in Burslem, Staffordshire. Operating under an agreement with Wood & Sons (see p.76), Radford produced vases, jugs, plaques, mugs, teapots, bowls, posy baskets, cigarette boxes, and ashtrays, as illustrated in the 1940 catalogue, left.

Decoration
Floral and foliate patterns were hand-painted in various colour combinations in mainly underglaze soft colours.
* Popular patterns include Anemone (best-known), Michaelmas Daisies, Blossoms on Bough, and Indian Tree.
* Geometric patterns with gold or silver trim are more unusual and therefore more expensive.
* Radford specialized in stippled backgrounds applied by hand in blue, pink, fawn, or green (as seen in the main picture).

C. T. MALING & SONS

Chinese Lanterns wall plate by Maling
1937; value code G

Identification checklist for Maling decorative art wares
1. Is it made of earthenware?
2. If it is a wall plate, does it have tube-lined decoration?
3. Is the decoration hand-painted in bright colours?
4. Does it have a floral pattern with a lustre glaze?
5. Is there a striking contrast between the colour of the ground and the decoration?
6. Does it have the Maling Ware castle mark?

C. T. Maling & Sons
Established in 1857 in Newcastle-upon-Tyne, Tyne and Wear, by 1889 the pottery was trading as C. T. Maling & Sons. By 1909, Maling's had two huge potteries and claimed to be one of the largest earthenware manufacturers in the world. During the early decades of the 20thC, Maling developed the range of keenly collected brightly coloured hand-painted and lustre ware for which the company, which closed in 1963, is best known today.

Decorative wares
In 1908 Maling launched Cetem Ware – dinner, tea, and breakfast wares, and toilet services in a white, china-like semi-porcelain body aimed at the middle-class markets. As production of Cetem Ware expanded, so too did Maling's decoration department, under the direction of Harry Clifford Toft, who built up a team of skilled paintresses, stencillers, and blowers, who applied background colour with pressurized guns. Following Toft's death, the new head designer C. N. Wright was joined in 1926 by the decorator Lucien Boullemier, and together they introduced a new class of decorated wares marked with the Maling Ware castle.

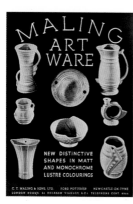

Wall plates

One of Maling's most successful ranges was a series of large wall plates with distinctive bright colours and raised tube-lined decoration, seen in the main picture.
* Decorative themes were very varied, ranging from the Oriental-inspired designs shown left to images of windmills and flowers.

Patterns and shapes

The general trade depression of the late 1920s and '30s encouraged diversity, and Maling's introduced a number of new Jazz Age wares and patterns.
* New patterns included a zigzag Tango border design; the dramatic Anzac geometric pattern teaset (1931); the stylized Tulip pattern (1932); and Anemone.
* New shapes included the Art wares shown in the 1937 advertisement above, and the Ritz-shape vase.

* The more traditional floral pattern shown on the ginger jar (c.1930) below left remained popular and was widely used on a range of shapes.
* The marked colour contrast between the deep-blue ground and the bright pink and yellow flowers on the floral dish (c.1928) shown below is typical of Maling's decorative wares of the 1920s and '30s.
* Other ranges included commemorative wares, and blue-and-white wares, often made for tea companies.

Lustre wares

Wedgwood's success inspired Maling to produce its own lustreware ranges of ornamental jugs, vases, boxes, etc, in a wide variety of shapes and patterns.
* The metallic surface is produced by using metal oxides,

usually silver or copper.
* The wares were decorated with printed and enamelled floral decoration in pastel colours with an iridescent glaze.

Collecting

The decorated wares of the 1920s and '30s are the most collectable, quality and condition of decoration dictating value.
* Large wall plates are eagerly collected but must be in perfect condition.
* Wall plates with less common coloured grounds, such as pink and blue, are rarer and more sought after.
* Maling lustre wares are the other important collecting strand. Again quality, condition, and in particular, decoration, will determine value.
* All Maling wares are collectable in North East England, where they tend to fetch higher prices.

DEVON POTTERIES

Cottage ware teapot by Torquay Terracotta Co.
c.1955; value code I

Identification checklist for Devon potteries wares
1. Is the piece made of red earthenware?
2. Does it have slip decoration in bright or contrasting colours?
3. Does it have a *sgraffito* motto?
4. Is it made in a traditional form?
5. Is it possibly made as souvenir ware?

Devon potteries
In the mid- to late 19thC a handful of small potteries set up in South Devon to make fine terracotta wares from local high-quality red clay. Most of their wares were aimed at the burgeoning tourist market and included jugs, vases, flower pots, teapots and teasets, candlesticks, money boxes, and other novelty items. Many were decorated with slipware and *sgraffito* mottos and became collectively known as Devon motto wares.

Decoration
Slipware decoration had been associated with the West Country, and North Devon in particular, since at least the 17thC and was readily adapted for souvenir wares in the 19thC. Typically the reddish brown "redware" earthenware bodies were partially covered with white slip and decorated with *sgraffito* mottos and hand-painted or printed motifs in traditional styles.
* Royal Devon Art Pottery (est. Exeter, 1894–mid-1930s) used mottos, and ship, bird, and cottage motifs on a variety of brown earthenware forms, as shown in the advertisement of 1914, top of p.73.
* Torquay Terracotta Co. (est. Torquay, c.1875–c.1939) was one of several South Devon companies who used the country-cottage motif, seen in the main picture, on motto wares.

C. H. Brannam
Brannam (est. Barnstaple, 1879; see p.17) was one of the leading manufacturers in South West

England of slip-decorated art pottery, novelties, and souvenir motto ware.

* Brannam's slip-decorated art-ware range (early 1880s–c.1938) was called Barum, the Roman name for Barnstaple.
* The imaginative designs, in soft colours and with adventurously fluid decoration, as seen in the fish-and-seaweed decoration on the Barum Ware vases bottom p.72, made 1904, show a hint of Art Nouveau.
* Brannam also made domestic and tablewares in bright colours, notably blue.

Honiton Art Potteries

In 1918 Charles Collard took over the Honiton Art Potteries (est. Honiton, 1881–1992) and introduced a range of exceptional hand-painted pottery that was influenced by Poole wares (see p.62).
* Collard pieces were made from local clay.
* The decoration was hand-painted – predominantly in blue, red, green, and purple – on a white or tinted opaque glaze.
* The designs were largely Jacobean- or Persian-inspired.
* All pieces are finished with a hand-dotted edge.

Later Honiton wares

In the 1950s, under the direction of Norman Hull, the developing range of Collard designs became the main area of production. Several new lines were introduced, alongside giftware, although high-quality hand-painted designs remained the company's forte. The fine

charger shown below, made in the early 1950s, is decorated with Sweetcorn, a pattern designed and applied to the piece by Jessie Banbury, which has elements, such as the Persian flowers and hand-dotted edge, derived from Collard's designs.

Collecting

Souvenir wares are an increasingly popular niche collecting area.
* Pieces with unusual mottos and town names are especially popular, but good condition is essential.
* Earthenware chips easily, so check carefully for damage on vulnerable areas.
* Damage to surface decoration will dramatically reduce value.

* Collectors prefer traditional decoration and forms.
* Vases in traditional patterns are among Honiton's most collectable products.
* Other popular and collectable manufacturers of motto ware include Aller Vale (est. Newton Abbot; c.1887–1962), Longpark (est. Torquay; c.1903–57), and numerous other well-documented factories.

WADE

A selection of Disney animal models and figures by Wade 1950s; value codes H/I each

Identification checklist for Wade animal figures
1. Is it made of porcelain?
2. Does it have hand-painted detail?
3. Is it well-modelled in an interesting pose?
4. Does it feature an endearing animal or a character from a Disney film?
5. Does it still have its original box?

Wade
From 1935, A. J. Wade Ltd and Wade, Heath & Co. traded as Wade Potteries. In 1958 Wade Potteries and George Wade & Son merged and traded under the name Wade Potteries. The diverse groupings produced a very wide range of pottery, from tableware through to the animal and nursery figures that are now keenly collected.

Tablewares
In the early 1930s, Wade, Heath & Co. produced a range of moulded, embossed, and hand-painted wares similar to the Carlton Ware range (see p.58).
* The dish right has an element of novelty in the inclusion of the small fish.
* Other moulded dishes featured more typical motifs, such as one

with hollyhocks and lupins and another with cobnuts.
* Moulded tablewares must be in perfect condition.

Harmony range
The Harmony range (1956–early 1960s) shown top p.75 featured strange shapes with pierced circular decoration.
* Fruit bowls on feet, hourglass vases and jugs had different decoration and colourways.

characters in earthenware.
* Mickey, Minnie, Pluto, and Horsecollar were brought out as a boxed set with a Mickey Mouse label.
* By 1935 Mickey Mouse tea sets of 8, 10, and 16 pieces were in production.
* Snow White and the Seven Dwarfs were other early figures.
* The Hat Box series featured characters from *Lady and the Tramp* (see examples in the main picture).

* Transfer-decorated Harmony is more eagerly collected than two-tone pieces.
* Two-tone colour combinations included grey and pink, shown here, and green and peach, and a dramatic green and black.
* Transfer patterns included Shooting Star (very popular in the 1950s), Parasol (rarer and more collectable), and Carnival.

Modern wares

The Zamba range of c.1957 featured adventurous shapes in black-and-white decorated with bold black decorations of lively tribal dancers.
* The range included ashtrays, jugs and vases, such as the one shown below.
* The unusual shapes were prone to hairline cracks, and the black enamel on the inside is liable to craze and eventually peel and may have been inexpertly repainted.

Disney ranges

In 1934 Wade acquired the rights to reproduce Mickey Mouse

Other animals and figures

A vast range of new animals and figures was produced after WWII, including:
* a range of 21 Nursery Rhyme figures in 1953;
* the first boxed set of George Wade miniature Whimsies – a fawn, a horse, a poodle, a

squirrel, and a spaniel – in 1954;
* the Wade Minikins range of 48 miniature models;
* the Nat West pig family ("Baby" is shown above), designed to encourage young people to start saving, in the 1980s. These are now collectable, especially in the form of sets.

Marks

Figures are not always marked and do not have serial numbers. Use a specialist collectors' guide (see p.185) to identify and date figures.

WOOD & SONS

*Piazza Ware vase by Wood & Sons
late 1950s; value code I*

Identification checklist for Wood Piazza Ware
1. Does it have a 1950s contemporary look?
2. Does it have an unusual asymmetrical organic shape?
3. Does it have a matt finish?
4. Is it hand-painted?
5. Is it decorated with an abstract pattern?

Wood & Sons
Established in 1865, the company traded as Wood & Sons from 1910, merging in the 1930s with H. J. Wood, which had been founded as an independent company c.1884. By the early 20thC the company was one of the largest and most progressive businesses in the Burslem area,

producing mainly dinner, tea, toilet, hotel and badged ware, and fancies for the middle and mass markets.

Utilitarian wares
Wood's was best-known for its ranges of utilitarian but good-quality single-colour wares used in hospitals, cafés, and homes across Britain. They conformed to wartime restrictions (see

PRESENTING 'Piazza'

A NEW RANGE OF
STYLISH GIFT WARE
CREATED BY
H. J. WOOD LTD

This new range of attractive gift ware in
stylish contemporary design has an immediate appeal to the discriminating customer.
We look forward to receiving your trade
enquiries at the

GIFTS & FANCY GOODS FAIR
Room 287, Imperial Hotel, Blackpool
Feb. 6th—9th

H. J. WOOD LTD · BURSLEM · STOKE-ON-TRENT. *London Showroom: R. H. WHEATLEY, Room 193, Audrey House, Holborn, E.C.1*

p.118) and are still in production
* Among the best known are Beryl, Jasmine, and Iris.
* Beryl Ware, introduced in the 1930s and shown on the bottom of p.76 in an advertisement from the 1940s, was made from Wood's standard green body and remained in production throughout WWII.

Ringwood Ware
Ringwood Ware, introduced in the 1950s, was a development of Wood's utilitarian ranges.
* Shapes were more rounded, organic, and streamlined.
* The characteristic Ringwood ridges, seen at the top of the Hedgerow tea-for-two teapot shown bottom p.76 strength-ened the shape and were both practical and decorative when applied to the edge of saucers, the bases of cups, and the rims of jugs and sugar bowls.
* Ringwood came in a variety of patterns and colourways, from the stylized natural printed and hand-coloured pattern shown here to brightly coloured polka dots and designs such as Carnival in abstract shapes.

Designers
Under the shrewd directorship of Harry J. Wood, the company employed several distinguished designers. Frederick Rhead, art director from 1912, created designs for domestic tableware and developed new ornamental artware, including now highly collectable early tube-lined designs. Susie Cooper (see p.124) collaborated with Wood's, initially buying in their blanks,

and, in 1931, relocating her pottery to Wood's Crown Works. Edward Radford (see p.69) worked for Wood's before setting up an independent pottery under an arrangement with Harry J. Wood. Charlotte Rhead (see p.127) worked briefly for the company

Giftware
The Piazza giftware range, launched in 1956, included vases, ashtrays, bowls, and toast-racks in both abstract and figurative designs.
* The fluid shapes were influenced by contemporary American designs.
* The matt finish was a fashionable "hand-crafted" detail.
* The hand-painted graphic patterns, shown in the main picture and above, were influenced by modern abstract art.

Later wares
Tableware has remained one of Wood's staples. The Holly Cottage dinnerware below, c.1990s, has a range of classic shapes decorated with a pattern reminiscent of the work of Eric Ravilious (see p.129).

ROYAL CROWN DERBY

Rose-painted wares by Royal Crown Derby
1900 to 1930; value codes H/I

Identification checklist for Royal Crown Derby
1. Is it made of porcelain?
2. Is the decoration hand-painted?
3. Is the decoration fine quality?
4. Does the decoration include gilding?
5. Does the decoration echo traditional or Oriental styles?

Royal Crown Derby
Established in 1876 in Derby, Derbyshire, Crown Derby became Royal Crown Derby by permission of Queen Victoria in 1890, when the company had become hugely successful, due mainly to its superb hand-painted and gilded porcelain. The range of figures, tableware, and ornamental ware in largely traditional forms and decorative styles continued throughout the 20thC. In 1973 Derby became

part of the Royal Doulton Tableware Group (see p.80), but is now independent again.

Imari patterns
* Derby's first Imari-style patterns for tablewares date from the 1760s and have been popular ever since.
* Each pattern has its own name; well-known examples include Old Witches, Cigar, and King's pattern.
* The company's range of highly collectable miniature Imari pieces includes toy saucepans, milk churns, and casseroles.
* Over the years the pattern has been adapted and applied to other popular ranges such as paperweights (see the Imari Honey Bear, 1990s, left).

Other patterns
In the 20thC leading decorators applied a range of traditional floral patterns to tableware, decorative ware, and fancies. Roses were a favourite motif and, as seen in the main picture,

were used in combination with gilding to cover the entire piece, or in less dense patterns (including garlands and swags) that highlighted the fine quality of the porcelain body. Sèvres-inspired designs often used white panels with floral decoration on a dark, richly coloured ground. Many patterns were also printed.

* Desiré Leroy, Derby's most accomplished decorator, trained and worked at Sèvres, joining the company in 1890.
* Cuthbert Gresley and Albert Gregory, both famous for their flower painting, produced much of Derby's hand-painted wares in the 1930s.

Wares
By 1946 Derby was producing figures, statuettes, and fancies such as the traditionally styled boxed examples shown right in the advertisement of 1954. In the 1970s the sculptor Robert Jefferson modelled new ranges of figures and a series of highly successful animal and bird paperweights that are now collectors' items.

* The first six paperweights were launched in 1981.
* The range is expanding, and Jefferson's early Cat, Rabbit, Hedgehog, Duck, and Badger have been remodelled.
* Some of the more collectable figures by Jefferson include *Les Saisons*, The Great Lovers (Antony and Cleopatra, Shakespeare's Romeo and Juliet, Lancelot and Guinevere, and Robin Hood and Maid Marion).

Influences and collecting
Many of the 20thC shapes and decoration were inspired by traditional Derby forms and 18thC Sèvres porcelain. The teaware set above, for example, although made in the 1990s, has a Regency-influenced shape decorated with a traditional Imari pattern.

* Prices for Royal Crown Derby have risen strongly in recent years, especially for cabinet pieces signed by well-known decorators such as Desiré Leroy,

and for certain niche areas such as Imari miniatures and paperweights.

* Pieces are nearly always clearly marked and these marks are rarely faked. However, other factories have copied many Derby-stle Imari patterns, and some of these have also used Derby-style marks.

ROYAL DOULTON I

*Sung and Chang flambé ware by Royal Doulton
1920s; value codes G/F*

Identification checklist for Doulton Sung and Chang flambé Ware
1. Is it made of porcelain?
2. Is it made of stoneware? (Chang Ware)
3. Is it thickly potted? (Chang Ware)
4. Does it have an Oriental-inspired form?
5. Is it decorated with a rich red glaze (Sung and flambé wares)?
6. Or is it decorated with multicoloured glaze (Chang Ware)?
7. Does it have a crackled effect glaze (Chang Ware)

Royal Doulton
Established in Lambeth, South London, in 1815, in 1902 the company became Royal Doulton. Production from its two factories in Lambeth and Burslem, Staffordshire, spanned the whole range of pottery and porcelain. Charles Noke, a talented modeller who had trained at Worcester, was art director from 1914 and played a major part in the company's success. He experimented with new glazes and forms launching popular ranges that reconciled art and design with the demands of the popular market place.

Tablewares
In the early 20thC Doulton acquired a new reputation as maker of high-class painted and gilded porcelain with dessert ware such as the plate, p.81 top left, made in 1916. Called The Close of Summer Day, it was decorated by J. H. Plant, who also painted seascapes, historical landscapes, and studies of animals, game birds, and fish. Other distinguished artists employed on this range included Edward Raby, David Dewsberry, and Percy Curnock.

By the 1930s, Royal Doulton responded to the success of

Clarice Cliff's Art Deco pieces with its own range of tableware in elegant, Modernist styles and hand-painted Art Deco patterns.
* Popular patterns include Tango, Gaylee, Athlone, De

Luxe, Syren; popular shapes include Envoy.
* The Iris teaware trio below was also made with a solid flower-shaped handle used on a luxury model from 1934. Cups with such typically Art Deco details are more eagerly collected than those with the "open 7" handle shown below.
* In general tablewares produced after c.1938 are less desirable, although some 1950s and early '60s designs are quite stylish.

Flambé wares

With Noke's encouragement, and the help of Bernard Moore (see pp.17–18), Doulton produced a successful high-temperature reduction-fired flambé glaze that led to the production of popular flambé ranges that swept the board at the 1904 St Louis Exhibition.
* The flambé glaze is made from copper, usually deep crimson, flecked with blue or purple, and often faintly crackled, as seen on the pots (main picture). It is

reduction fired, i.e. in an atmosphere with reduced oxygen.
* Sung Ware, inspired by early Chinese ceramics, was made in a variety of colours and exotic decoration. Veined Sung Ware had a randomly patterned glaze.
* Chang Ware is more experimental, richly glazed, and dramatically coloured.
* These ranges were very popular in the 1920s, when exotic Oriental-inspired forms and glazes were very fashionable.
* The designer Harry Nixon specialized in Sung, Chang, and flambé wares, and his mark H Nixon generally appears on the side of the piece.

Bunnykins nursery ware

The original Bunnykins patterns, launched 1934, were based on the drawings of Barbara Vernon Bailey, daughter of Cuthbert Bailey, general manager at Doulton's from 1925. They were inspired by her childhood in rural Shropshire and her father's bedtime stories and have remained perennially popular.
* By WWII 66 designs were in production, applied to a range of

traditional nursery wares like the pottery plate above, made in the 1950s.
* In 1939 Charles Nokes designed six Bunnykins figures and a modelled tea set.
* Bunny-shaped wares included teapots, egg cups, sugar sifters, and jugs.
* Later additions to the range include 20thC preoccupations such as television, jogging, and space travel.
* Earlier discontinued designs and shapes are now most collectable, together with pieces produced until the 1950s with Barbara Vernon's signature.
* Doulton also made other nursery and children's ranges.

Royal Doulton figure of The Bather by Leslie Harradine
1920s; value code H

Identification checklist for Doulton Art Deco figures

1. Is she moulded in bone china and hollow inside?
2. Is the decoration hand-painted?
3. Is the subject a realistic "modern" woman?
4. Is she a typical "English Rose" with fair colouring and rosy rounded cheeks?
5. Does she have pale flesh tones?
6. Is the subject shown in a casual pose?
7. Is it marked ?

Character and Toby jugs

In 1934 Charles Noke revived the Staffordshire Toby jug tradition with a range of Toby jugs and character jugs based on famous figures from British history, literature, and folklore that are now a major collecting area.

* Toby jugs are full-length figures; character jugs, showing just head and shoulders, were often made in four sizes.
* The first character jug was John Barleycorn, modelled by Charles Noke.
* The handles of character jugs are modelled to reflect the subject, as seen in the

Captain Hook jug shown here, made in the 1960s.

* Rarity and character rather than date have the biggest impact on value. Among the most collectable are Harradine's Dickens' characters, and unusual variations, such as the Alfred Hitchcock jug with a *Psycho* pink shower curtain handle (versions with a blue curtain are more common).
* A short production life makes a jug more collectable.

Figurines and modellers

First introduced in 1913, the famous Doulton figurine range was the staple output of decorative wares during the 1920s and '30s and continues to be one of the prime collecting areas. Charles Noke, art director from 1914, recruited a team of distinguished modellers. Leslie Harradine (1887–1965), one of the most prolific and famous, produced numerous popular designs, including The Bather (main picture), made in several versions, including a nude, and various colourways.
* Other well-known modellers were Albert Toft, Phoebe Stabler, Charles Vyse, and Peggy Davies.

with an all-weather surface to create large fountain and garden figures, like the Lily Maid c.1930 below.

Other modellers have continued to add to the thousands of different figures, many based on fictional characters, such as the model of Elizabeth Bennet (below left), the heroine of *Pride and Prejudice*, made in the 1990s, which continues the tradition of fine modelling and hand-painted detail.

Condition

The exposed limbs of figurines are particularly vulnerable and are parts most likely to have been restored.
* Look and feel for subtle changes in skin tones and surface glazes where retouching may have occurred.
* Enamels, particularly blacks, were unstable and prone to flaking and may have been over-painted.
* The bases were cast with the figure and sometimes have stress cracks. These will not detract from value provided they do not extend more than 1in (2.5cm) from the hole underneath the base or to visible areas of the piece.

Marks

* Figures from the 1920s and '30s have a hand-painted factory mark; other figures usually have a printed mark.
* The HN factory reference number (hand-painted until the 1950s) gives the title and records when the piece was introduced and withdrawn.

* The early figures produced before 1917 and the Art Deco figures, many of which were produced in runs of only 2,000, remain rare and valuable.
* From 1924 the sculptor Gilbert Bayes used the newly developed Doulton polychrome stoneware

ROYAL WORCESTER

*Figure by James Hadley for Royal Worcester
1910; value code G*

Identification checklist for Royal Worcester figures by James Hadley
1. Is it made of porcelain?
2. Is it finely and naturalistically modelled?
3. Is it hand-painted?
4. Does it have a distinctive blush ivory or old ivory finish?
5. Does it feature an idealized figure in a rustic setting or, alternatively, an Oriental or other exotic Eastern figure?
6. Does it have a moulded Hadley signature on the base?

Modellers
From the 1930s the freelance modeller Doris Lindner created

many fine horse models, such as the American Saddle Horse left, made in 1970. Other designs included a range of thoroughbred and individual horses. These highly detailed models were produced in limited editions and are popular with American collectors.

James Hadley (d.1903), senior modeller at Worcester, worked in many different styles.
* His figures, many in Oriental- and Eastern-inspired forms, are keenly collected.
* One series (see main picture) was given a blush ivory finish – soft tints of ivory and pink –

that echoed contemporary glass finishes and was copied by German and Austrian manufacturers.

The sisters Freda (d.1972) and Dorothy (1892–1962) Doughty were leading modellers in the 1930s.

* Dorothy designed the American Birds and British Birds series. Launched in 1933, they were known as Doughty birds and produced until the 1970s.

Porcelain tableware
The high-quality tableware produced in the latter part of the 20thC was decorated with both historical and contemporary patterns. The egg coddler shown above has been a perennial favourite since its launch in 1890. This example of 1990 is decorated with Hanbury, a design based on 18thC blue-and-white ware.

* Other well-known patterns include Evesham, a fruit pattern used for both kitchen and oven-to-tableware.
* The Worcester Herbs pattern shown on the oven-to-tableware below, made in the 1990s, was inspired by botanical drawings. It was used on tableware, oven-to-tableware, giftware, and accessories.

Worcester Royal Porcelain Company
The original 18thC Worcester factory, a pioneer of English porcelain, fragmented into several companies before regrouping as Worcester Royal Porcelain in 1862. At the beginning of the 20thC, Worcester still produced grand ambitious porcelain painted by generations of new famous artists, which, together with a range of well-modelled and naturalistically painted ceramic sculptures produced throughout the century, remain the prime collecting area.

* From 1890 decorators were allowed to sign their work. Well-known and collectable artists include Harry Davis (1885–1970), and the Stinton family of John (1854–1956), Harry (1883–1968) and James (1870–1961).
* Some other well-known and collectable painters would include Walter Sedgley (act. 1889–1929) and Walter Austin (1891–1971).

SPODE

Blue Italian pattern jug by Spode
1990s; value code I

Identification checklist for Spode
1. Is the piece made of earthenware?
2. Is the form traditional?
3. Does it have an underglaze transfer-printed pattern?
4. Is the pattern derived from traditional blue-and-white ware?
5. Is it marked Copeland Spode?

Spode
Established in 1776 in Stoke-on-Trent, Staffordshire, Spode was bought by W. T. Copeland in 1833, and either Copeland or both names were used jointly until 1970, when the company reverted to the use of Spode. Tableware has remained the backbone of production, largely in traditional shapes and patterns that have remained perennially popular, such as the underglaze blue-and-white printed ware shown in the main picture.

Patterns
Spode production has remained on the Church Street site since the factory was first established, allowing the company to build up an enormous archive that holds over 70,000 tableware patterns. As a result, designers

have tended to rely on the past for inspiration.
* The Blue Italian pattern

shown in the main picture (with mark on p.87), is still a best-seller. It was created in 1816 and has been in production ever since. It is believed to have been based on a drawing from 1690.

* Spode has produced blue-and-white printed ware from the late 18thC. It still produces some of

its original chinoiserie patterns from hand-engraved copper plates.

* Patterns are now printed by lithography.

Blue-and-white transfer-printed ware

This type of decoration was applied to utilitarian domestic pieces and was inexpensive to produce, using underglaze blue transfer-prints taken from engraved copper plates and needing only one firing. after the biscuit firing. Different copper plates had to be created for each size and form, and sometimes designs are oddly adapted to fit more unusual shapes. Earliest patterns, such as the ubiquitous Willow Pattern, were inspired by Chinese ceramics.

Tablewares

After the take-over in the mid-19thC Copeland expanded production to include lavish painted and gilded porcelain in the French style. The Sèvres-style plate (bottom p.86), made in 1906–07, was a copy of a Sèvres original and formed part of a set ordered by Tsar Nicholas II to match a service commissioned by Catherine the Great in 1776. The same tendency for Spode to follow or copy success-ful design styles continued to a great extent throughout the 20thC.

* In the 1930s the designer and modeller Eric Olsen created a range of vases, bowls, jugs, and other wares in contemporary fluid forms in pastel colours and matt glazes that were not unlike Keith Murray's Modernist range for Wedgwood (see p.121).

* The 1950s two-tone tableware below had the fashionable soft colours, often made by using tinted slips over a white body, that had been started by Poole (see p.63) and developed by Wedgwood. The Spode shapes remain traditional.

* More original in both shape and decoration was the Cutie Kitten wares children's range designed by Christopher Boulton in the 1950s. It featured a cat in numerous poses associated with sports, such as the oarsman shown on the plate above left, made c.1958.

* The unusual coupé triangular shape, decorated with contemporary images, was used for the Barbecue series, introduced in 1957 and designed specifically with informal entertaining in mind.

* The award-winning Royal College tableware shape, designed by Neal French and David White, was launched in 1960.

JOSIAH WEDGWOOD I

A Fairyland Lustre ginger jar by Wedgwood
1920s; value code E

Identification checklist for Wedgwood Fairyland lustres

1. Is it made of porcelain?
2. Does it have an Oriental shape?
3. Is it decorated with a fantasy-inspired landscape peopled by elves, fairies, and other imaginary characters?
4. Does it have a variegated dark-coloured ground printed with bright colours and gilding?
5. Does it have a lustrous metallic sheen?
6. Is it signed?

Josiah Wedgwood & Sons
Josiah Wedgwood, who established his pottery at Burslem, Staffordshire, in 1759, was the first potter to commiss-

ion leading artists for designs. The tradition continued throughout the 20thC and collectors focus on distinctive designs, often by well-known modern designers.

Designers
Alfred and Louise Powell, designers for Wedgwood from 1906 until (in Alfred's case) the early 1940s, set up a studio where they trained paintresses to paint the whole pattern freehand, rather than use the restrictive printing and hand-colouring technique.
* Following the success of the freehand-painted wares at the Paris Exhibition of 1925, a small

handcraft studio was established at Etruria in 1926.

* It was run by Millicent Taplin, one of the Powell's protégées, assisted by girls from Burslem School of Art.

* The Cane Ware vase below, made c.1928, was designed and painted by Taplin and has her monogram. It was probably a prototype for Wedgwood's Sun-lit pattern and other Art Deco-inspired patterns produced by the new handcraft studio.

Victor Skellern, art director from 1934, was Wedgwood's first fully trained professional designer.

* He introduced technological developments such as silkscreen and lithographic printing.

* The china coffee set designed by Skellern in 1935, shown bottom of p.88, features the Persian Ponies pattern – one of a series of handcraft china patterns from the 1930s.

Lustre wares

In the 1920s Wedgwood produced a range of lustre wares whose success encouraged companies such as Carlton (see p.56) to produce similar pieces.

* The Fairyland lustre wares designed by Daisy Makeig-Jones (see p.10 bottom left), were both the most popular and most expensive.

* The fantastic landscapes and elves, pixies, goblins, etc, who inhabited them looked back to the turn of the century, but the bright colours and shapes, as seen in the ginger jar in the main picture, had a modern feel.

* Fairyland lustre wares are marked on the base with the letter Z and a pattern number.

* Daisy Makeig-Jones also designed the Chinese and Butterfly lustre wares and some children's wares.

Commemoratives and limited editions

Wedgwood has a reputation for highly collectable commemorative and special editions, in both traditional and modern styles (see p.120).

* Souvenirs from the Festival of Britain, 1951, include Norman Makison's mug, now very rare and collectable, with contemporary graphic designs featuring the Skylon and the Dome of Discovery.

* Mugs celebrating the Coronation of Queen Elizabeth II in 1953 were designed by Richard Guyatt, who used the traditional Wedgwood Queen's Ware body, and, now highly sought after, Eric Ravilious, whose design for the Coronation of Edward VIII was re-drawn (see p.129).

* Well-known artists were commissioned for series of limited-edition plates (see p.34).

* The Jasper 1998 Christmas

plate below is one of a popular series introduced in 1969. Jasper Ware was inspired by antique cameos and first introduced c.1767. Blue was always the most commonly found colour, but the early blue was either a very deep purplish blue or a slate blue rather than the pale "Wedgwood" blue shown here.

JOSIAH WEDGWOOD II

A Monkeys group animal model by John Skeaping for Wedgwood late 1920s; value code E

Identification checklist for John Skeaping animal figures for Wedgwood
1. Is the piece a stylized animal model or group?
2. Is the body cast in Queen's Ware or black basalt stoneware?
3. Does it have a matt or semi-matt glaze in cream, celadon, tan, or white?
4. Is it marked with an impressed Wedgwood stamp and an incised J. Skeaping mark?
5. Does the model reflect the influence of contemporary sculpture?

Nursery ware
In 1949 Wedgwood acquired the sole reproduction rights for Beatrix Potter characters from Frederick Warne & Co, first publishers of her highly popular children's books.
* The range includes standard nursery wares such as mugs, plates, and bowls, money boxes, soap dishes, egg cups, and lamp bases.
* Beatrix Potter nursery ware continues to be highly popular, and additions to the range include the clock plate, shown right, made c.1990.
* In 1937 Eric Ravilious (see p.129) created Alphabet nursery ware. Transfer-printed designs of capital letters on bands of pastel colours such as pink, yellow, or

grey, with black-and-white illustrations beneath each letter were applied mostly to standard tableware shapes.

Wedgwood and Modernism
Norman Wilson, works manager

from 1930, was largely responsible with Tom Wedgwood for turning the theory of Modernism into practice at the Wedgwood factory through his experiments with new glazes, developing many of the new matt and satin glazes and

coloured slips and celadons used by John Skeaping and Keith Murray (see p.121).
* From 1926 Skeaping (1901–80) designed a successful, and now very collectable, range of stylized animal figures in the new glazes (see Monkeys group, main picture).
* Early and most collectable

versions usually have a matt glaze and are impressed with the Wedgwood mark and John Skeaping's name.
* Later reissued editions have a high-gloss glaze and are marked with the company stamp only.

The slip-decorated vase shown left, with its clean Modernist lines and striking Art Deco-inspired design, is part of the Unique Ware range designed by Wilson.
* The word "Unique" refers to the glaze effects, many of which were created by Wilson, who also designed some of the shapes used exclusively for this range. Wilson's protégé Victor Skellern (see p.89) continued the new design lines with such talented designers as Robert Minkin, who worked for the company from 1955 until 1986.
* In 1963 Minkin designed the stoneware coffee set shown below.
* The tall, straight-sided cylinder shapes epitomize 1960s style.
* The traditional black basalt glaze looks stylish and contemporary.
* The clean lines, minimal decoration, and understated elegance reflect the contemporary Scandinavian influence.

T. G. GREEN & CO.

Cornish Ware by T. G. Green & Co
1920s; value code I

Identification checklist for T. G. Green Cornish Ware

1. Is the piece made from white earthenware?
2. Is it a piece of kitchenware, domestic ware, or tableware?
3. Does it have raised coloured bands, probably blue but perhaps yellow, or other colours?
4. Are the bands sharp-edged, showing that they were turned rather than moulded?
5. Does it have a Cornish Kitchen Ware mark?

T. G. Green & Co.
T. G. Green & Co. was established in 1864 in Church Gresley, Derbyshire. By 1905, the company had become a major enterprise, producing a great variety of wares. The early ranges of kitchen and tablewares are now eagerly collected.

Cornish Ware
First introduced in the 1920s, Cornish Ware was an immediate success and in 1928 was awarded Britain's Certificate of Hygiene.
* The white earthenware body was dipped into coloured slip and a lathe used to cut bands through the colour to reveal the white body beneath, leaving the coloured bands in relief.
* Colourways include blue – most common and most popular; yellow, introduced in the 1960s; and later greens and other colours.
* Most familiar are the storage jars and covered caddies – more than 100 printed contents names have been recorded.
* Rarer items include toast

racks, lemon squeezers, and egg separators.
* Shapes of pieces such as coffee pots reflect the changes in fashion.
* Cornish Ware had a major shape redesign in the 1960s by Judith Onions.
* It is still being produced in the original factory.

Tablewares

The Blue Domino Ware pattern (late 1930s–mid-1960s) was made by applying paper dots to the body of the piece, and spraying blue slip over the top. The paper dots were then removed to leave a recessed polka dot pattern and the piece was then fired.
* The biscuit jar, bread-and-butter plate, and toast rack, bottom p.92, are unusual examples of 1950s Domino and are therefore popular with collectors.
* In 1993 there was a revived version of Blue Domino using Cornish Ware shapes.

Contemporary influences

The Gingham on Patio range (1950s), shown below, combined both modern pattern and shape.
* The pattern derived from the newly popular gingham fabrics was used on the full range of Patio kitchen and tableware.
* The Patio Modern shape, based on square forms, with softened square cups and jugs, reflected the influence of the American "new look". The Fleur pattern used on the casserole and plate (right), made in the 1960s, reflects the influence of Scandinavian

design (see pp.172–73).
* The graphic and stylized pattern of flowers and herbs is reminiscent of Picknick, one of the most popular patterns used by the Swedish company Rorstrand.
* The border pattern is formed by simple black prints that are then hand-painted.

Collecting

The striped, spotted, and gingham patterns are now classics and keenly collected.
* Inferior copies of Cornish Ware are being produced. Authentic pieces can be identified by the

raised coloured bands.
* Due to its popularity fakes of Cornish Ware are now being produced. In particular look out for jars with rare labels that have been applied later.
* Later Cornish Ware should not be confused with the earlier, more collectable, wares.
* Modern pieces have a heavier body. Most shapes are different, and reflect the remodelling of the range in the 1960s. They do not have the church shield mark.

MIDWINTER I

*Hugh Casson designs for Midwinter
late 1950s; value code H/I*

Identification checklist for 1950s tableware by
Midwinter
1. Does the piece have a modern organic shape
reflecting American designs?
2. Is it made of earthenware?
3. Is it decorated with an abstract or stylized graphic
pattern?
4. Is the decoration inspired by contemporary textile
designs?
5. Or, alternatively, does the decoration reflect the
1950s interest in foreign travel and food?
6. Does it have a printed or painted pattern?

W. R. Midwinter
Founded in 1910, W. R.
Midwinter was already a
significant pottery in Stoke-on-
Trent before WWII. But it was
after the war, when Roy
Midwinter (1923–90), son of the
founder, became design director,
that Midwinter became one of
the most prolific and innovative
producers of stylish, contemporary and well-designed
tableware of the 1950s and '60s.

Designers
Midwinter drew on the talents
of a range of freelance designers.
The architect and watercolourist
Hugh Casson had never
designed for china before, but
his delicate and charming
illustrations, inspired by the
south of France, became the
highly popular Riviera (1954)
and Cannes patterns, shown in
the main picture decorating
a range of Fashion shapes.

The Chequers plate above (1957) was designed by Terence Conran (b.1931), whose other successful patterns include Nature Study, and the popular Plantlife.

The in-house designer Jessie Tait (see p.128), created shapes as well as imaginative, mainly abstract, patterns for both the Midwinter Modern ranges.

* Many of her pattern designs were textile-inspired, in particular Homeweave and the black-and-white striped Zambesi pattern, seen on the Fashion tureen (bottom p.94).

* Other popular 1950s patterns by Tait include Red Domino and Festival. The latter was inspired by the Festival of Britain in 1951, and the molecular images were one of the first patterns to be hand-painted on to the new Fashion range.

* Zambesi, which spawned a host of imitations, was made using underglaze black stripes and on-glaze red enamel. A less expensive and less collectable version was produced without the red detailing.

* Zambesi tureens show off the radical new Fashion shape to perfection and are keenly collected.

* Zambesi tea and coffee ware is now increasingly collected.

Midwinter Modern

The Stylecraft and Fashion shapes were influenced by the organic ceramic designs of Eva Zeisel (see p.166), whose work Roy Midwinter had seen on a research trip to the USA and Canada in the 1940s.

* The cube-shaped Stylecraft Coupé tableware, launched c.1952, was backed by extensive advertising.

* Stylecraft was decorated with a range of patterns, mostly abstract or stylized and hand-painted in underglaze acid-proof colours.

* The Stylecraft trio shown below, made c.1954, is decorated with the Primavera pattern, inspired by contemporary textiles and designed by Jessie Tait.

* The Fashion shape (various examples seen in the main picture), designed by Roy Midwinter and William Lunt and launched in 1955, included over 50 pieces with flowing lines in which the rim disappeared, and projecting elements such as handles, spouts, lips, and knobs became graceful free-flowing shapes that harmonized with the main body.

* Pieces were designed for multi-use: for example the oatmeal dish could also be used for fruit or soup.

MIDWINTER II

Coffee ware designed by David Queensberry for Midwinter 1960s; value codes I

Identification checklist for 1960s tableware by Midwinter
1. Is it made of earthenware?
2. Does it have a tall, straight-sided cylinder shape?
3. Does it have a vertical-striped pattern in muted 1960s colours; or alternatively a psychedelic-inspired pattern in blues and greens; or perhaps a Pop Art- inspired pattern?
4. Do the shapes reflect Scandinavian design?
5. Is it marked?

Later Midwinter designs
The company was as innovative in the 1960s and '70s as it had been in the 1950s, introducing a new range of shapes and patterns that captured the new design styles and the spirit of the times. In 1962, the company launched the Fine-shaped tableware, shown in the main picture above, designed by David

Midwinter
FINE TABLEWARE
STAFFORDSHIRE ENGLAND
SHAPES DESIGNED BY THE
MARQUIS OF QUEENSBERRY

Queensberry in collaboration with Roy Midwinter.
* The straight-sided cylinder shape was a typical 1960s feature.

* The straight sides provided a good surface area for pattern, making it perfect for decoration.
* The Sienna pattern shown in the main picture, designed by Jessie Tait, was one of the most influential patterns on the new cylindrical teaware, and, together with the Queensberry pattern, started the 1960s trend for patterns in vertical stripes. Other popular "striped" designs include Mexicana and Piccadilly.
* Other popular 1960s patterns were more psychedelic in inspiration, such as the hugely popular blue and green Spanish Garden pattern by Jessie Tait (see p.128).

However, not all the new Midwinter 1960s shapes and

patterns were successful. The MQ2 shape, designed by Roy Midwinter and David Queensberry and based on a chemist's bottle, and the Portobello shape, were both commercial failures and were withdrawn.

The MQ2 teapot shown below was made in 1967, a year before the ill-fated shape was withdrawn. The transfer-decorated Pierrot pattern, designed by Nigel Wilde, makes the best of the rather limited amount of space on the rounded lower body and low-slung spout. Ironically, one of Wilde's other designs, a Pop Art-inspired pattern known as Diagonal, had to be withdrawn from production because it was so

difficult to adapt to fit the different Fine shapes.

1970s Midwinter
In the 1970s the cylinder shape that had dominated the 1960s was modified, as seen on the Caprice teapot on p.96. The cylindrical geometric area of the body was reduced, the handles became larger and more curving, tops became rounded and the decoration more relaxed and freer.
* The blue and green colour combination remained popular, as seen on the Caprice teapot, a pattern influenced by Jessie

Tait's highly successful Spanish Garden (see p.128).
* Floral patterns became increasingly popular, reflecting the preoccupation with ecology.
* Colours became softer and more earthy, as in the Autumn pattern of poppies and seed heads, which is rare and therefore more sought after and expensive.

The Stonehenge range, launched in 1972, captured the current back-to-the-land and self-sufficiency ethos and reflected the impact of studio ceramics. Roy Midwinter designed the shapes and his wife Eve Midwinter was involved with the Creative matt glaze patterns.

The Sun pattern plate (above), had a bright orange sun at the centre; the Moon plate (above) had a white moon surrounded by midnight blue bands; and the Earth plate had a white centre surrounded by thick bands of brown.
* Other ecologically inspired ranges were the Stoneware shape, designed by Robin Welsh, introduced in 1979.
* The patterns for Stoneware were designed by Eve Midwinter and included Natural, Hopsack, Denim, and Blueprint.

Collecting
Many of the patterns from the 1960s were made in huge quantities, so collectors are looking for rarities. These include:
* biscuit barrels and sugar sifters with chrome accessories;
* shapes and patterns made for a limited period, such as MQ2, Portobello, Diagonal, and Mediterranean patterns.
* Tablewares can still be found in charity shops and car-boot fairs, but prices are rising.

PORTMEIRION POTTERIES

Magic City pattern coffee pot by Portmeirion
c.1966; value code I

Identification checklist for 1960s Portmeirion
coffee sets
1. Is it made of earthenware?
2. Does it have a tall, cylindrical, straight-sided shape?
3. Does it have an embossed textured surface, or
perhaps an intricate printed pattern, or a humorous
design inspired by 19thC advertising catalogues?
4. Does it have a printed dark-coloured oval mark,
with the factory and designer's name reversed out in
white?

Portmeirion Potteries
Susan Williams-Ellis and her
husband Euan Cooper-Willis
began trading as Portmeirion
Potteries in 1962 from London
Road, Stoke-on-Trent. In 1960
they bought the small pottery-
decorating business of A. E.
Gray & Co. (see p.48) and in
1961, Kirkham Potteries, and
the two companies were
combined and named after
Portmeirion, the famous Welsh
seaside village designed by
Susan's father, the architect
Clough Williams-Ellis. Susan
Williams-Ellis's first designs
were made by Gray's to sell in
the souvenir shop in Portmeirion

in the 1950s. In the 1960s she
began designing shapes as well
as patterns, and Portmeirion
became well known for its
innovative ceramic tablewares
and is still popular today.

Early designs

Early souvenir wares for the Portmeirion shop included copper-plate reproduction prints in plain black and white, and the Dolphin storage jars, decorated with printed labels engraved from Susan's own drawings.
* The Dolphin design was later sold through Gray's, and, from 1960, by other stockists. Black-and-white examples made in the 1960s are more readily found.

Early designs for Gray shapes included the Moss Agate range.

This unusual process was developed by Susan Williams-Ellis. These expensive pieces (see beaker above, c.1960) were decorated with engraving overlaid with rich gilding.

Portmeirion wares

The Kirkham works provided 19thC copper engraving plates and moulds that Ellis adapted for an innovative and hugely successful range of tea and coffee wares in particular.
* The cylindrical moulds produced tall straight-sided coffee pots, such as the Serif shape (1964, main picture) and the Cylinder shape.
* These shapes were perfect canvases for innovative decoration, from the popular printed Magic City pattern shown in the main picture, to a range of embossed designs, such as the Jupiter pattern shown at the bottom of p.98.
* The Totem pattern, launched in 1963, was an unusual embossed design with a coloured translucent glaze. Produced in amber brown (now most commonly found), light-blue, pale green, pewter, and white (rare and highly collectable), it was an immediate success and was widely imitated.

Floral patterns

The Botanic Garden design, based on early 19thC floral prints and launched in 1972, was an instant success and remains Portmeirion's flagship pattern.
* The range now includes some 160 items, a few of which are shown below.
* A new collectable range of Botanic Garden includes a hinged-box collection of enamelled copper and china boxes launched in 1996.
* Floral ranges remain perennially popular, and in 1994 new ranges were launched including Welsh Wild Flowers, Summer Garland, and Ladies' Flower Garden.

RIDGWAY POTTERIES

Homemaker coffee pot by Ridgway
1955–67; value code I

Identification for Homemaker wares by Ridgway
1. Is it made of earthenware?
2. Is it decorated with a graphic black-and-white printed pattern based on modern home furnishings of the 1950s?
3. Does it have a Homemaker Ridgway Potteries mark?

Ridgway Potteries Ltd
From 1879 in Shelton, Staffordshire, the firm produced a wide range of tablewares. In the 1950s Ridgway's developed a truly distinctive style with its Homemaker range.
* It was designed by Enid Seeney (b.1932), who used a textured hatched background combined with a stylized graphic illustration of contemporary fashionable home furnishings.
* It was intended as cheap and cheerful domestic ware for young couples setting up a new home and sold in huge quantities exclusively through Woolworth's from 1955 to 1967.
* Flatware and cups and saucers were made in huge quantities and are readily found.
* Rarer and more sought-after pieces include milk jugs, tea and coffee pots, which were decorated with cut-outs of the illustrations.

* Other popular pieces include the coupé vegetable dish, oval platter, and steep-sided 1950s-style cereal bowls.
* A rare and collectable rust-coloured version was produced for export only.
* Homemaker's success inspired several similar designs, such as the Fiesta pattern seen below, made in the early '60s as part of Barker Bros, Royal Tudor Ware, and Fantasia by Burgess & Leigh (see p.54).

RYE POTTERY

*A selection of Rye Pottery wares
1950s; two-handled vase, jug, avocado dish,
cruet set, value codes H/I*

Identification checklist for Rye 1950s domestic wares
1. Is it made of thick earthenware with a white tin-glaze?
2. Does it have a hand-thrown traditional shape?
3. Does it have on-glaze hand-painted decoration?
4. Is the decoration brightly coloured with abstract surface designs?
5. Do the patterns show the influence of Scandinavia and 1950s Poole Ware?
6. Is the piece marked?

Rye Pottery

The Pottery was founded in Rye, East Sussex, in 1947, by the brothers Walter and John Cole, both sculptors and studio potters. Though the factory made some studio ceramics, its stock-in-trade in the 1950s was a range of affordable, and now collectable, original artistic domestic wares.
* This was shown at the Festival of Britain in 1951 and sold through stores such as Heal's in London and Tiffany in New York.
* The Cottage Stripe pattern above was used on hand-thrown and cast shapes and has been in almost continuous production since 1947.
* Early Cottage Stripe pieces have dark-red clay bases and often an impressed pottery mark; later pieces have a Made in Rye, England backstamp.
* By the 1960s there were some 250 designs and colourways.

Other 1950s and '60s wares

The Rye studio wares, influenced by Scandinavian design (also seen on '50s Poole ware), textiles, and contemporary studio wares, moved away from the influence of Leach into decorative Modernism. Typical motifs include stars, dots, stripes, and *sgrafitto* decoration.
* Throughout the 1950s Rye made a series of miniature pieces often too small to be marked but decorated in the distinctive style, with soft primary colours and spiral patterns used on coasters, plates and other wares.
* Tankards were produced in a variety of shapes and styles. Hand-thrown ones are prone to damage, but if so may still be worth collecting for display only.
* Today the pottery is known for its hand-painted figures.

DENBY POTTERY

Glynbourne Ware designed by Glyn Colledge for Denby c.1960; value code H

Identification checklist for Glynbourne Ware
1. Is it made of stoneware?
2. Is it hand-thrown?
3. Do the pieces look handcrafted?
4. Is the decoration hand-painted in broad brush-strokes?
5. Is it an all-over pattern depicting stylized foliage in soft greens and browns?
6. Does it have a matt glaze?

Danesby Ware
The generic name Danesby Ware was used for Denby's art pottery until the 1960s.
* Orient Ware (see vase p.103 left, c.1926), and Electric Blue are the most easily found and popular of 1930s Ware.

The popular 1930s Pastel decorative ranges included Pastel Blue (below c.1933), and Regent Pastel (c.1933), and had semi-matt glazes and moulded relief decoration of flora, fauna, and typical Art Deco subjects.
* A series of ornamental nursery wares was introduced in 1934, including bookends (now popular and collectable) and modelled animals. Glyn Colledge designed some of Denby's most successful, and now collectable 1940s and '50s ranges.
* The 1940s GlynWare range was typically decorated with stylized hand-painted leaf patterns, often in dark greens and earthy browns. The New Glyn Ware of the mid-1950s featured white earthenware curving bowls and dishes

with leaf decoration.
* Glyndebourne (1948–50)
hand-thrown vases, jugs, bowls,
and lamp bases had horizontally
ribbed surfaces decorated with
soft pastel shades.
* Glynbourne, designed 1960–61
(see main picture), was a prestige
line of large hand-thrown bowls,
vases and jugs reminiscent of
fabrics of the time.

Tablewares

The Denby stoneware body was
perfect for oven-to-table wares.
One of the earliest tablewares
was Cottage Blue, with a rich
blue mottled glaze and yellow
interior. Introduced in 1926 on
traditional shapes, it is still
popular. Some of the other
earliest ranges were by Donald
Gilbert, who designed the Epic
(introduced 1933) and Manor
Green ranges.
* Manor Green (introduced
1938–39) was reintroduced in the
1950s and made until the 1980s.
The Greenwheat oven-to-table
range was designed by Albert
Colledge. Made from 1956 until

1976, it was one of Denby's
most successful lines.
* The design, shown on the
platter below (1955), was entirely
hand-painted with its own
backstamp.
* Greenwheat was a popular
export design selling to the US,
Australia, and New Zealand.
* The pattern was used on a
variety of shapes; hollowware
pieces have rich dark-green
glazed interiors.

Tigo Ware

Tigo Ware, launched in 1956
and shown above, was created by
Tibor Reich (b.1916), a freelance
Hungarian designer.
* The stark black-and-white
designs were worked on an
imported white clay earthenware
body rather than the stoneware
traditionally used by Denby.
* The range included decorative
plates and vases as well as
tableware.
* The black, lightly textured
matt-glazed surface was
decorated with *sgrafitto*

technique to expose the white
body underneath.
* Most collected today are the
4-piece Mustar condiment set,
the Rendezvous and the Sisters
plate, and the coffee pot and the
cocoa mug.

SHORTER & SON

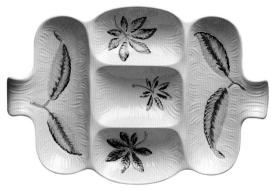

Hors d'oeuvre dish by Shorter
1950s; value code I

Identification checklist for 1950s wares by Shorter
1. Is it made of moulded earthenware?
2. Is it hand-painted?
3. Does it perhaps have an embossed fruit
and flower design?
4. Is it marked?

Shorter & Son
Trading as Shorter & Son from
1878 in Stoke, Staffordshire, the
pottery made almost exclusively
majolica and associated products
– ornamental useful ware,
fancies, and novelty items with
low-relief moulded or embossed
decoration – until about 1927.
The 1930s was a period of
diversity, and the company
became well known for its many
ranges of decorative fancies and
ornaments in both traditional
and contemporary styles for the
popular market and tablewares.
These were updated again in the
1950s, and such 1930s and '50s

wares are the main focus for
collectors today. In 1964
Shorter's was taken over by S.
Fielding & Co., and shortly
afterwards Shorter patterns
and shapes appeared with
Crown Devon backstamps.

Figurines
Clarice Cliff (see p.122)
collaborated with Shorter's in-
house designer Betty Silvester
on a range of Gilbert and
Sullivan figurines based on
D'Oyly Carte actors in Gilbert and
Sullivan operettas.
* Shorter obtained permission
from the D'Oyly Carte Opera

Company to model jugs from five Gilbert and Sullivan operettas.
* The concept was extended with the issue of figurines. The series above, based on *The Mikado*, was designed c.1940 but not produced until 1949.

1930s wares and designers

Diversity was the key note of Shorter's production at this time. The Stag Ware vase shown below right, made in the mid-1930s, was a more traditional design that looked back to Victorian majolica. Such designs were given a more contemporary look, as shown here, with one of the series of new soft-matt glazes that were introduced in 1936.
* A radical departure from traditional production was a series of five vases – Thisbe, Pyramus, Rhomboid, Noni, and Olwen – in Modernist shapes and pastel glazes made in the early 1930s.

Mabel Leigh joined Shorter & Son as a designer in 1933 and helped to revolutionize the pottery's output during her short stay.
* She designed hundreds of shapes and reinterpreted traditional cottage ware with her Shantee and Pagoda ranges.
* Her main creation was the Period Pottery, shown bottom p.104, with the Khimara pattern, for which she designed both the shapes and patterns.
* This colourful and decorative range had modern freehand-painted and *sgraffito* decoration inspired by traditional European, Middle Eastern, and African sources.

1950s wares

In the 1950s Shorter's wares followed contemporary trends as they had done in the 1930s.
* A range of white matt-glazed vases was introduced.
* Many of the earlier hand-painted embossed fruit and flower designs were revived in new colourways, and two new series, Harmony and Petal, were introduced.
* The ornamental range was adapted to include contemporary shapes and patterns for less formal dinnerware, as shown by the hors d'oeuvre dish in the main picture.

Collecting

Many enthusiasts collect all types of Shorter products.
* Rarities and figurines fetch the highest prices.
* Some of Shorter's majolica tablewares, such as Strawberry & Bow (later renamed Pompador) and Cherry Ripe remained popular throughout the firm's existence.

Marks

* Marks usually incorporate the Shorter & Son name.
* The "GENUINE STAFFORDSHIRE" printed mark (see below) was introduced in the 1940s.

CHINTZWARE

Du Barry chintzware by James Kent
1940s; value codes H/I

Identification for chintzware
1. Is it made of earthenware (although some pieces are made of china)?
2. Does it have an all-over transfer-printed floral pattern?
3. Is the pattern based on textiles?
4. Do the shapes reflect their production period, for example, squared plates?
5. Is it marked?

Chintzware

Chintzware was first produced in the 1920s and '30s, when it was intended as affordable tableware, in particular teaware, for everyday use. The fresh and pretty patterns were produced on transfer sheets and applied to an extensive range of shapes, usually with a matching, or on de luxe versions, gilt trim. Particular skill was needed to cover irregular surfaces and avoid obvious joins. Several major British manufacturers produced their own ranges.

James Kent (est. 1897)

James Kent produced chintz and floral patterns from the 1920s onwards.
* The Du Barry pattern, shown in the main picture, is perhaps the company's best-known chintzware pattern.

* It was reintroduced in 1998 on the Square Diamond shape.
* In the 1960s Kent launched the Rosalynde chintzware pattern, based on the English moss rose.

Royal Winton

Royal Winton, the trade name of Grimwade Bros (est. 1886, Stoke; from 1979 part of Howard Pottery Group), became renowned for its chintzware in the 1930s, producing a range of patterns that are now keenly collected. Hazel, seen on the four-cup Ajax-shape teapot illustrated at the top of p.107, is one of the top patterns.
* Other sought-after patterns include Evesham, Julia, Royalty, Sweet Pea, and Welbeck.
* Rare shapes include teapots, hot water jugs, lamp-bases, candlesticks, and biscuit barrels.

* Toast racks were especially difficult to decorate, and on later, less collectable versions, the bars are sometimes left plain.

Crown Ducal

Crown Ducal, a trade name of A. G. Richardson, produced another highly popular early chintzware range. The Peony pattern tray shown below was made in the late 1920s. In terms of collecting, its large size and attractive fluted edge help compensate for the scratch on the surface. Such damage will reduce value but is preferable to restoration in the form of hand-painting or use of another similar pattern.

* Crown Ducal's Ivory Chintz, made in the 1920s, was one of the earliest chintzware patterns and features a bird hidden among the flowers.

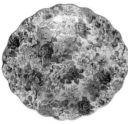

* Primrose was another popular pattern, usually produced in blue and yellow. There are some very rare pink and green versions

with an orange trim, but they may have been samples.

Other manufacturers

In 1954 Kensington Pottery (est. 1922, Hanley, Staffordshire) launched Summertime and Blossomtime, two transfer-decorated chintz teaware ranges that blended 1930s and '50s styles.

* Shapes included teapots, sugar bowls, egg sets, and a Cosy Set, consisting of a rectangular teapot and hot-water pot on a tray.

This biscuit barrel was part of Midwinter's (see p.94) chintzware range. It is decorated with the Springtime pattern (also known as Brama), one of the company's most collectable patterns that was made in the late 1920s and the '30s.

Identification and marks

Many chinztware patterns are very similar, and it can be difficult to identify them and distinguish between them. Manufacturers used a range of marks, some of which, like the Royal Winton mark (see left), give the pattern name. Other patterns can be checked in one of the many excellent chintzware reference books (see p.185).

Collecting

Chintzware is now eagerly collected worldwide, especially in the US, and prices reflect this.

* The condition of the pattern is crucial: clean, clear, brightly coloured, crisp-looking patterns ensure maximum value.
* Fading, scratches, obvious join lines, or insertions of other patterns will detract from value.
* Patterns on lids and bases should match exactly if original. Look out for "married" pieces.
* Several patterns have been re-introduced.
* Due to its popularity many collectors' clubs exist.

HORNSEA POTTERY CO.

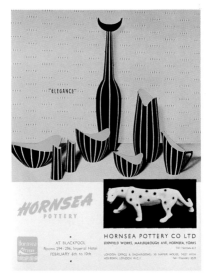

Elegance tableware accessories by Hornsea
1956; value codes I

Identification checklist for 1950s Hornsea tableware accessories
1. Is it made of earthenware?
2. Does it have a distinctive, well-designed contemporary shape?
3. Does it have striking decoration, often in relief, that complements the form?
4. Does it reflect Scandinavian influence?
5. Is it marked?

Hornsea Pottery Co.
Hornsea Pottery was founded in 1949 by the brothers Desmond and Colin Rawson in their home in Hornsea, East Yorkshire. By 1954 they had acquired new premises and a 64-strong workforce that produced modern slipware, contemporary-shape vases, tableware accessories, and fancies. In the 1970s Hornsea acquired a second factory in Lancaster, Lancashire, and a growing reputation for well-designed, well-crafted contemporary earthenware. The Pottery has since closed, following financial difficulties.

John Clappison (b. 1937)
John Clappison first produced designs for Hornsea in the late 1950s, while still an art-school student. He later became design director and was largely responsible for creating Hornsea's modern image.
* In the 1950s he designed the successful Elegance range, shown in the main picture, with its bold contemporary shapes highlighted by the equally dramatic black-and-white decoration.
* He caught the mood of the 1960s with the Studiocraft range. Made from 1960 to 1962, Studiocraft pieces had their own logo and ranged from the black-and-white Op Art-patterned planter shown top p.109, to a range of delicate pieces, with

relief spikes or dots, finished with a matt creamy-white glaze, such as the Thorn vase.
* In the 1970s, Clappison's kitchen storage jars, shown below, captured the fashionable country-kitchen back-to-nature style with traditional shapes and the Saffron pattern with its earthy brown tones.
* Clappison's work is attracting considerable interest and may be more difficult to find than other Hornsea wares.

Decoration
Hornsea was one of the pioneers of direct printing, at that time an unusual way of screen-printing a resistant substance directly on to biscuit ware. In the later stages of glaze dipping and firing, the glaze runs off the screen-printed decoration and produces the effect of glazed areas of one colour and contrasting semi-matt areas in another colour, as seen on the Saffron storage jars below.
   The Rainbow pattern, with its distinctive ridges, was decorated by hand, which meant that no two pieces were the same. Planters were a popular range and the one shown above right, made from 1961 to 1963, was, like other Hornsea planters, produced in a variety of colourways and in a number of different sizes.

Tablewares
Hornsea's reputation for good design was firmly established when its Concept tableware received the Design Council Award in 1977. Designed by

Martin Hunt and Colin Rawson, the modern 1970s shapes have a hint of 1930s streamlining.
* Concept was extremely popular but was largely exported to the US and Canada and so can be difficult to find in Britain.
* It was produced in various colours: cream, matt black (Image, see top p.14), grey and pink (Swan Lake), and in a short-lived pale-blue glaze (Cirrus).
* Martin Hunt also designed Hornsea's Contrasts tableware. This successful range of bold, modern two-tone ware was introduced in 1975.

Collecting
* Hornsea pottery is very prone to flaking and chipping. On some larger shapes this is acceptable as fewer were made.
* Other ranges, such as the Home Decor range by John Clappison, must be in perfect condition.
* Collectors should concentrate on contemporary and Modernist styles.
* The mark below was introduced in 1951.

TROIKA POTTERY

Anvil vase by Troika
1960s; value code H

Identification checklist for Troika ceramics
1. Is it made of moulded earthenware?
2. Does it have a textured surface?
3. Is it decorated with abstract designs?
4. Are the colours earthy and muted?
5. Do the shapes and decoration reflect the
influence of the Cornish landscape?
6. Does it have a hand-painted mark on the base?

Troika Pottery
The pottery was founded in
1963 in St Ives, Cornwall, by
the sculptor Lesley Illsley, the
potter Benny Sirota, and the
architect Jan Thompson to
produce artistic but saleable
pottery. Early production was
small decorative items, but larger
sculptural pieces (many now
sold through auction houses)
were made as the pottery
expanded. In 1970 Troika
moved to Newlyn, and continued
production a further 13 years
but closed in 1983.

Decoration
Unconventional production
methods produced interesting
tones and textures reflecting
colours, textures, and forms
of the Cornish landscape.
* Early decorative wares were
either textured or finished with
a distinctive smooth white glaze.
* Many of the later, larger
designs, such as urns, spice jars,

vases, and lamp bases had
sculptural or architectural
shapes, such as the anvil-shaped
vase shown above.
* Patterns were often worked
on different layers, with abstract
motifs reflecting the influence
of paintings by Ben Nicholson
and Paul Klee.
* The textured surfaces often
imitated stone and slate.
* The colour range was muted
(shades of grey, brown, creams,
and white), but freely applied.

Collecting
* Jam pots and small cylindrical
and round vases are common.
Quality of decoration affects
price, with a clean graphic image
or popular Egyptian symbol
adding to value; pieces with
minimal decoration are less
valuable.
* Large, sculptural or daring
shapes are very collectable and
highly priced, especially those
inspired by Ancient Egypt.

J. & G. MEAKIN

Manderley coffee pot by Jessie Tait for J. & G. Meakin c.1969; value code I

Identification checklist for J. & G. Meakin 1960s Studio range
1. Is it made of earthenware?
2. Is the coffee pot tall, slender, and cylindrical?
3. Does the flatware have a border pattern and central motif?
4. Does it have distinctive, contemporary semi-abstract printed graphic decoration?
5. Is it marked with a Studio backstamp?

J. & G. Meakin
Established in Stoke-on-Trent in 1851, by the 1950s J. & G. Meakin were producing a range of modern tableware. The Studio Ware shape with coupé plates launched in 1953 (see top p.12) was inspired by Russel Wright's American Modern (see p.168). In 1964 the company launched another Studio line,

designed by Tom Arnold. It was probably its most successful and fashionable range, and, following Meakin's takeover of Midwinter in 1968, was often decorated with striking designs by Jessie Tait (see p.128), such as the Manderley pattern shown above.
* Other popular and collectable Tait patterns include Impact (in fashionable blue and green), and Inca (in a typically 1970s brown and orange colourway).

Alfred Meakin, brother of James and George Meakin, also produced tableware throughout the 1950s. The plate, left, is typically decorated with on-glaze transfers depicting light-hearted escapist scenes of everyday life such as outdoor cafés, the seaside, and fairgrounds. Other patterns include My Fair Lady, The Gay Nineties, Jivers, and cowboy items inspired by Hollywood westerns.

111

KITCHENWARE

Cobblestone kitchenware by C. T. Maling & Sons
1930s; value codes I

Identification checklist for 1930s kitchenware
1. Is it made of earthenware?
2. Does it have a traditional form?
3. Does it have a high gloss glaze?
4. Does it have a clean crisp pattern, usually white combined with a strong colour?
5. Is it made in an extensive range of functional shapes with related patterns?
6. Is it made in several different colourways?

1920s and '30s kitchenware
The burgeoning production of attractive kitchenware in the 1920s and '30s was driven by social change such as fewer servants and modern, hygienic kitchens. There was also a market for accessories that harmonized with the new surroundings. Mixing bowls, baking dishes, pitchers, storage jars, butter dishes, rolling pins, cruet sets, sugar sifters, measuring jugs, lemon squeezers, egg separators, etc, were made in large quantities,

usually in traditional shapes, but with bright new patterns and colours.

Manufacturers
T. G. Green's Cornish Kitchenware (see p.92), launched in 1925, was hugely successful and widely imitated.
* British Anchor Pottery Co. (1884–1982) produced banded Cottage Green kitchenware shown below in 1939.
* C. T. Maling & Sons (see p.70) Cobblestone kitchenware range (main picture) typically uses

traditional forms and fresh-looking patterns that combine white with a strong contrasting colour.

Later kitchenware

Shapes remained largely traditional but the decoration reflected contemporary trends. The mixing bowl below, made by Price & Kensington in the 1950s, came with a matching rolling pin and measuring jug. The bright colours and graphic abstract pattern were inspired by contemporary textile designs.
* Price & Kensington also produced a banded kitchenware

range, including storage jars, closely based on Cornish Ware (see p.92) and advertised as ideal for "the modern housewife".
* The popularity of decorative kitchenware in the 1950s prompted even smaller manufacturers such as Kirkham to make popular ranges, including patterns such as Spots and Stripes (1959–62), used on a wide variety of shapes including sifters and preserve pots, and Chef-and-stripe (1959–62), a bold red and yellow pattern that combined a naive stickman in a chef's hat with "cocktail stick" lettering naming every piece.
* Kirkham's domino pattern can be confused with the popular Midwinter Red Domino tableware range, launched in 1953, but the Kirkham pattern is used on shapes such as rolling pins and storage jars that were not part of the Midwinter range.
* Kirkham was taken over by the Portmeirion Pottery in 1962 (see p.98) and some Kirkham patterns will have a Portmeirion backstamp.
* Pountney's Pottery of Bristol Pottery's Long-line kitchenware won the *Good Housekeeping* magazine's seal of approval. The white bodies were decorated with graphic engraved illustrations of cutlery; lids were in bright primary colours.

* Other popular ranges include Bretby's blue-and-white KK range, and later T. G. Green patterns (see p.92).

The ceramic canisters shown below were made by Crown Devon (see p.60) in the 1960s. The stylized daisy motif and bright reds and oranges were both highly popular at the time, as was the lower-case typeface and the flat lids.
* In the late 1960s and very early '70s bold, colourful graphics were used on patterns such as Gaytime that featured on kitchenware by the Lord Nelson Pottery.
* 1970s kitchenware was made in more muted colours, often with textured surfaces, such as the Hornsea storage jars on p.108.
* Oven-to-tableware kitchenware was increasingly popular and major manufacturers such as Poole (see p.62), Midwinter (see p.94), and Denby (see p.102) produced successful ranges of casseroles decorated with contemporary patterns such as Denby's Gypsy – a giant dusky-pink rose pattern launched in 1971.
* From the late 1970s many kitchenwares are marked "dishwasher proof" and "freezer and microwave safe".

Collecting

Kitchenware is readily found and must therefore be in good condition.

* Pattern rather than form usually dictates collectability, although rarer shapes such as lemon squeezers or egg sep-arators are sometimes collected.
* Storage jars are very popular as the shape offers a good surface for decoration and is less prone to damage. Original lids are essential.
* Kitchenware is often popular because it is still usable and fits in with modern kitchen styles.

NURSERY WARE

Fortune Telling tea set group by Paragon
1920s; value code G

Identification checklist for Paragon nursery ware
1. Is it made of moulded earthenware?
2. Is it decorated with a pattern designed to appeal to children, such as a nursery rhyme, illustrations of famous children's book characters, or popular cartoon or film characters?
3. Does it reflect its period?
4. Is there a related range – mug, plate, bowl, egg cup, baby's bowl etc?
5. Is it marked?

Nursery ware
Many major manufacturers produced nursery ware, much of which was based either on traditional nursery rhymes, or popular children's books, cartoon characters, films and, later, television programmes.

Paragon
In the 1920s and '30s Paragon was renowned for its nursery ware, such as the tea set shown in the main picture, designed by J. A. Robinson. In 1930, the then Duchess of York commissioned the Two for Joy magpie nursery ware for Princess Margaret based on the traditional rhyme.
* Eileen Soper's successful Children's China range led to further royal commissions.
* Other popular designs based on traditional rhymes included Mother Goose by Chloe Preston and the Tinker Tailor by Louis Wain.
* A Mickey Mouse series, launched in 1930, was based on story rather than pattern and was decorated with printed outlines that were then hand-coloured.

Shelley
Shelley first introduced nursery rhyme designs in 1902. The baby's plate shown right, made in 1916, has the characteristic stable thick-rimmed shape associated with children's bowls and popular nursery-rhyme decoration.
* The highly successful Mabel Lucie Attwell designs, commissioned from 1926 (see p.67), included cups and saucers, mugs, plates, teapots, napkin rings, and chamber pots. Most featured a verse and transfer-printed images.
* Attwell's nursery ware figures are particularly sought after.
* Other popular figures are the

Children at Play range designed by Hilda Cowham in 1924.

Famous designers
Susie Cooper's nursery range, although now eagerly collected,

was not a great success when first produced. The hand-painted decoration, as seen on the Chicken mug below, made in 1932, seemed rather crude in comparison with her other designs (see p.124).
* Cooper's nursery mugs were usually part of a porridge set that included a porringer and plate.
* The hand-painted design featured either a farm animal or one from the Noah's Ark range, and sometimes a child's name.
* The range was stamped with the Susie Cooper Production mark.

Wedgwood's successful Alphabet nursery ware range was commissioned from Eric Ravilious (see p.90), whose detailed and naturalistic graphic

design appealed to young children. Charlotte Rhead (see p.127) designed a range of children's mugs for A. G. Richardson.

Other manufacturers
* German and Japanese manufacturers mass-produced inexpensive lustred earthenware egg cups (see top right) for export in the 1930s. Typically they are unmarked, but novelty designs, such as rocking, whistling, or double egg cups, as well as those based on famous film or cartoon characters, are keenly collected.
   Classic children's books have inspired such collectable ranges as Ashtead's Christopher Robin service, produced in 1928 and designed by E. H. Shepard, the original illustrator of A. A. Milne's book, produced in 1928, and Grimwade's Peter Rabbit china teaware, launched in 1922, based on the Beatrix Potter book. In 1949 Wedgwood

acquired exclusive rights to reproduce Beatrix Potter's paintings and launched their own Peter Rabbit nursery ware (see p.90). Other collectable

nursery wares include:
* Royal Doulton's Bunnykins (see p.81)
* Poole nursery ware designed by Truda Carter (see p.126), and Dora Batty (1920s and '30s), Alfred Read (1930s), and Eileen McGrath (c.1934).
* Ranges based on Disney characters, such as that produced by Wade (see p.74) and Maw & Co. (1850–c.1970).

Television spin-offs
Television-inspired nursery ware is very collectable.
* The Andy Pandy Ware by Howard Pottery, shown below, launched in 1954 under the Brentleigh trade name, includes the traditional combinations of mug, plate, and bowl. Keele Street Pottery produced an inexpensive colourful lithographed range of Andy Pandy and Sooty mugs in the 1950s that were sold with confectionery.
* Other popular designs include the Magic Roundabout, Pinky and Perky, Bill and Ben the Flowerpot Men, and others.

The NEW Andy Pandy Ware for Children

Brentleigh

HOWARD POTTERY CO., LTD. Norfolk Street, Simton, STOKE-ON-TRENT

ADVERTISING WARES

Guinness Toucan by Carlton Ware
1960s; value code H

Identification checklist for Carlton Ware Guinness advertising wares
1. Is it made of earthenware?
2. Is it designed to stand on a bar-top or pub table-top? Or alternatively, is it a piece of domestic ware?
3. Does it feature a slogan, a motif, or an animal character specifically associated with Guinness advertising campaigns?
4. Is it brightly coloured? Or alternatively, is it produced in the black, white, and gold colour combination associated with Guinness?

Advertising wares
In the latter part of the 19thC pottery manufacturers made a wide range of advertising wares – bottles, jars, jugs, counter-top trays, pot lids, mugs, ash trays, etc, transfer-printed with advertising slogans.

Breweriana
Whisky-related items are the most popular collecting area within "breweriania". Doulton's Lambeth factory made some of the finest stoneware whisky crocks or jugs.
* Most whisky crocks were decorated with transfer-printed decoration.

* "Skirt"-shaped crocks that flare out towards the base, and mallet-shaped crocks with transfer printing, are unusual.
* Many whisky crocks were made for export to North America and Australia. The rare two-tone Rabbie Burns Whisky jar (bottom p.116), made by H. Kennedy of Glasgow c.1900–20, was found in Australia.

Water jugs

Jugs that advertised whisky and dispensed the accompanying water were made in many sizes, styles and shapes. Doulton's Barnsley Brewery jug (c.1906) is one of the finest examples,

promoting the Oakwell Brewery on the front, and two whisky distillers on either side.

Guinness advertising wares

In the 1950s Carlton Ware was commissioned to produce advertising ceramics for Guinness. The success of the Toucan character, originally created by John Gilroy (1898–1985) in 1935, launched a whole range of toucan-shaped or toucan-decorated wares, including condiment sets and flying toucans, that are now the most keenly collected of "Guinntiques".
* Best-known is the free-standing Toucan (see main picture), made in three sizes and also produced as a lamp base.
* Reproductions and fakes have been made so collectors should buy with care.
* A menagerie of ceramic bar-top animals, including kangaroos and tortoises, carrying the My Goodness My Guinness slogan was produced.
* Other Guinness wares include a 1960s Carlton Ware tea set with a black body decorated with white lettering and a gold harp;

and a lustre plate in black and white with a pink surround and central motif promoting Guiness.
* Carlton Double Diamond wares included the humorous jug left, typical of post-war advertising style. Such pieces have to be in perfect condition. The tightly fitting bowler hat is removable: if it is missing or damaged the price would be at least halved.

Smoking accessories

Pottery matchstrikers advertised both tobacco and other products on sale in the British pub, such as mineral water. Similarly, jugs and ashtrays advertising cigarettes and alcohol were also produced in quantity by a number of leading manufacturers. Shelley (p.66) produced an ashtray advertising Coates' Original Plymouth Gin; Wade's Carlsberg ashtray was decorated with a view of Copenhagen; other ashtrays advertised Black & White Scotch Whisky, featuring the black and white Scottie dogs; and White Horse Whisky.

Other manufacturers

Doulton was one of the major producers but many other potteries such as Grimwade, Pountney & Co, Shelley, and the

Staffordshire Potteries also made significant quantities of advertising wares. Beswick, which is well-known for its range of model animals (see p.45), made the large Dulux Dog (c.1964–70), seen above, for shop-window display that has now become one of the most popular and enduring advertising images.

UTILITY WARE

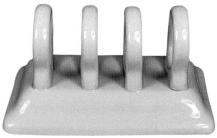

Utility Ware toast rack by Spode
c.1948; value code 1

Identification checklist for Spode Utility Ware
1. Is it made of high-grade cream or white earthenware?
2. Is the piece free of any decoration?
3. Is it a piece of essential functional tableware?
4. Are the shapes elegant and simple?
5. Is it marked with factory marks plus A, B, or C?

Utility ware
In 1942 the Domestic Pottery (Manufacture and Supply) Order restricted manufacture for the home market to specified essential undecorated types of earthenware and china that included cups, saucers, plates, jugs, mugs, beakers, pudding bowls, pie dishes, vegetable dishes, and teapots. These Utility wares were graded and marked A (white- or cream-body), B (glazed stoneware) or C (natural clay-bodies ware with a brown or colourless glaze)

according to price band. Several major manufacturers produced exciting new ranges of versatile and ingenious pieces that emphasized shape and design in the absence of decoration. Many companies closed or consolidated. Those with good export records were often licensed to produce more decorative wares for export, and others received government contracts for military Utility wares such as mugs, etc.
* Spode Utility Ware, shown in the main picture and the advertisement left, was made in high-grade cream earthenware. The teapot had a non-drip pourer, self-locking lid and built-in strainer.
* Wedgwood's white Victory Ware, designed by Victor Skellern, consisted of 18 pieces, several of which had dual functions, such as handleless-cups that could be used as sugar or slop bowls.
* The Bovey Pottery's War Ware also included novel features such as non-slip handles and multi-purpose shapes.
* Moorcroft (see p.52) produced a collectable Utility Ware range, as did several less well-known companies, but all had to be licensed to produce wares.

SOUVENIR WARE

Crested Forth Bridge by Arcadian Ware
c.1920; value code I

Identification checklist for Goss souvenir ware
1. Is it slip-cast?
2. Is it made of translucent parian ware?
3. Does it have on-glaze enamel decoration of a town or city crest?
4. Is it named on the base or the side?
5. Is it marked?

Souvenir ware
W. H. Goss was the first manufacturer to capitalize on the rapid growth of the tourist industry in the late 19thC, producing a range of small souvenir wares decorated with town and city crests that began a collecting craze. Crested ware could only be bought in the town or city whose coat-of-arms was depicted. Goss's success inspired many other potteries to produce their own ranges of crested wares that included miniature versions of whelk-shells, buildings and monuments, animals, different forms of transport, Welsh hats, Irish colleens at their spinning wheels, shoes, hats, household wares, and musical instruments, although these are rare.
* Goss pioneered the heraldic china market; the advertisement of 1926 right shows the company's use of miniature versions of historical models.
* Goss's very collectable range of 35 nightlight cottages were modelled on famous homes such as Ann Hathaway's cottage. Pre-1929 models are worth more than later models.
* Willow Art was the second most prolific manufacturer of crested ware and made a more varied range of coloured cottages than Goss.
* Arcadian Ware produced the best sports and pastimes range. Its vast range of pieces included

the Forth Bridge (c.1903–33), see main picture. It is most ornate and a good example of the firm's well-made models.
* Savoy China produced a particularly fine and rare range of musical instruments.
* The very few crested wares produced by Wedgwood, Worcester, and Royal Doulton are rare and much more valuable than those by more prolific firms, with the exception of Goss.
* Some of Shelley's best lines included animals; they may be marked Foley.
* Carlton made a consistently high-quality range that, like Goss, always used the correct coat-of-arms.

COMMEMORATIVE WARE

*Royal Wedding loving cup by Paragon
1981; value code H*

Identification checklist for Paragon royal commemorative wares

1. Does it commemorate in its decoration an important royal event – birth, wedding, coronation, or jubilee?
2. Is it made of china?
3. Does it have additional gilding?
4. Is it marked?

Commemorative ware

Most commemorative wares date from the mid-19thC, when improved methods of transfer printing reduced the cost of production.
* Rarity and quality of design will significantly affect appeal and value. Limited editions were often produced but are not necessarily more valuable.

* Vast quantities of 20thC royal souvenirs were made, and values remain low unless the piece is unusual or has been produced by a top manufacturer.

Manufacturers

* Paragon's royal commemoratives are very collectable: the Queen's Silver Jubilee Ware of 1997 sold out before it was made.
* The loving cup above with its fine china body and gilded details, is typical of Paragon's high-quality commemorative ware.
* The J. &G. Meakin Coronation mug left (1936) is a good example of how companies produced inexpensive commemoratives by using standard shapes and decorating them with stock transfers, many of which had been officially approved, bought from major suppliers and printers.
* Wedgwood commemoratives are the most collectable of all and include Coronation mugs by Eric Ravilious (see p.129), and by Richard Guyatt who designed a new Queen's Ware mug for the Queen's Coronation in 1953, and a tankard to celebrate the marriage of Princess Anne and Captain Mark Philips.

KEITH MURRAY

*Vases by Keith Murray for Wedgwood
1933–35; value code H*

Identification checklist for Keith Murray's ceramics
1. Does it have a pared-down Modernist shape?
2. Is the glaze monochrome and matt or semi-matt?
3. Is the body earthenware?
4. Is it marked?
5. Does it have incised, fluted, or annular ribbed decoration?

Keith Murray (1892–1981)
Born in New Zealand, Murray originally trained as an architect before becoming a notable freelance designer of glass and ceramics. From 1933 he worked for Josiah Wedgwood & Sons (see p.91), producing designs influenced by Modernist architecture that emphasized form rather than decoration, and designing the new factory at Barlaston. His designs include commemorative ware, tableware and tableware patterns, and small domestic items such as ashtrays, beakers, cigarette boxes, book-ends, candlesticks, and inkstands. His most sought-after designs are the range of bowls and vases, such as those in the main picture above, in distinctive Modernist shapes and monochrome glazes.

Vases and bowls
Murray's brief was to create designs specifically for mass-production by modern slip-casting. Vases and bowls were then decorated on an engine-turned lathe to give the distinctive ridges seen above.
* The black and copper basalt and red stoneware vases are rarest and most collectable.

Decoration
Murray used a distinctive range of new glazes with matt and semi-matt finishes, developed in the 1930s by Norman Wilson.
* Colours include semi-matt ivory-white Moonstone (1933); matt straw; matt green (both c. 1935); matt grey – used relatively rarely and withdrawn in 1940; and blue – also rare and collectable.
* Some glazes continued to be produced after 1940, including Moonstone, green, and straw.
* Surfaces often have incised horizontal or vertical decoration, annular ribbing, or fluting, as seen above.

Marks
Virtually all of Keith Murray's work is marked.
* Pre-war pieces have a full script signature on the base; black basalt wares have red marks.
* Pieces after 1941 have the initials KM and Barlaston mark.
* Many Keith Murray shapes were re-introduced in the 1950s.

CLARICE CLIFF

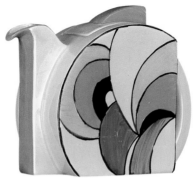

*Swirls pattern Bizarre teapot by Clarice Cliff
c.1932; value code G*

Identification checklist for Clarice Cliff Bizarre Ware
1. Is it made of earthenware with a distinctive "honey" glaze?
2. Does it have a geometric Art Deco shape?
3. Is it hand-painted?
4. Are the enamels laid on thickly, so that brush- strokes are visible?
5. Is the pattern brightly coloured and outrageously modern?
6. Does it have a Bizarre backstamp?

Clarice Cliff (1899–1972)
Clarice Cliff is probably the best-known English designer of Art Deco ceramics. In 1916 she joined A. J. Wilkinson's Royal Staffordshire Pottery, where she learned all aspects of pottery-making, including modelling, decorating, lithography, designing, and gilding. In 1927 Wilkinson's set her up in a studio in their newly acquired Newport Pottery with a team of paintresses, and in 1928 the hugely successful Bizarre Ware range was launched. By 1931 Clarice Cliff was art director and went on to design over 500 shapes and 2,000 patterns.

Shapes
With the earliest Bizarre pieces, Cliff's brightly coloured patterns were applied to Newport's stock of old-fashioned standard white wares. By 1929, her own range of matching geometric earthenware shapes was in production, as seen on the teapot above.
* The Conical range has cone-

shaped bowls, vases, sugar sifters, and tea wares with triangular handles or feet.
* Other popular shapes include Le Bon Jour, Stamford, Biarritz, and Lotus.
* Cone-shaped sugar sifters (prone to damage so check carefully) and beehive-shaped honey pots (check that lids match exactly) are popular.
* Geometrical shapes with solid or pierced triangular handles, and conical-shaped feet, are keenly collected today.

Patterns

Cliff's vast array of patterns, largely inspired by contemporary textiles and French flat-pattern folios, was applied to tableware, ornaments, and fancies.
* Early landscape patterns include a house or a roof, unlike later landscape patterns such as Coral Firs and the two rare further colourways: Blue Firs, and Green Firs.
* Crocus (late 1920s–1939) was one of the most popular patterns at the time and is therefore readily found and affordable. By 1934 it was available in various colourways: Spring (pastel pink, blue, and green flowers); Autumn (red, purple, and blue flowers); Sungleam (orange and yellow flowers); and the rarer Blue and Purple. Other popular patterns include Secrets and Nasturtium.
* Rare and desirable patterns include Gardenia, May Avenue, Appliqué, Inspiration, Sunray, Mountain, and Solitude.
* Designs of the late 1930s and 1950s in paler colours and with moulded details are not nearly so popular.

Ornaments

* Hand-painted wall plaques featured a variety of designs from geometric patterns to elaborate stylized landscapes, and floral and tree motifs. The Monsoon wall plate (c.1930) shown bottom p.122, is from the Appliqué series, one of the first to include individual pattern names with its own identifying mark.
* Clogs, or sabots, were inspired by Dutch clogs. Made in three sizes, they were designed to hold bulbs or cacti and decorated with a variety of patterns. They are not readily found today and are priced correspondingly.
* Vases are found in a myriad of shapes, sizes, and patterns, with unusual shapes or patterns (such as Inspiration, in blue and lilac) commanding a premium.
* The Age of Jazz figures are rare and highly sought after. They were reissued in the 1990s.

Masks

* Cliff face masks show the subject face-on rather than in profile.
* They were made in a variety of colours and sizes, with both matt and high-gloss glazes.
* They have hollow backs and are made with varying degrees of modelling to the face.
* Many feature various types of floral headdress, as seen on the Flora face mask (1932) below.
* All are keenly collected, in particular the rare Chahar.

Identification, marks, and fakes

The huge range and different combinations of shapes and patterns and marks have been catalogued in several specialist reference books (see p.185).
* The phenomenal success of Bizarre Ware spawned numerous

imitations, such as the Cubist jug below, 1930, by Crown Devon.
* Most but not all pieces are marked, and a variety of different marks was used.
* Hand-painted signatures and marks were phased out by c.1931 and replaced by stamped, and eventually, lithographed marks.
* Fakes are common. Tell-tale signs include washed-out "muddy" colours, an uneven,

slightly murky "honey" glaze, and a deliberately aged crackled glaze around the mark on the base.

SUSIE COOPER

Cubist pattern teaware by Susie Cooper
1930s; value code F

Identification checklist for early Susie Cooper tea
and coffee wares
1. Is it made of earthenware?
2. Does it have a typically geometric Art Deco shape,
with hand-painted decoration inspired by contemporary
abstract painting or textiles?
3. Or, alternatively, does it have a relatively traditional
rounded shape, with hand-painted or transfer
decoration of floral motifs, thick bands of bright
colour, or simple repeated patterns?
4. Is the decoration understated and precisely
executed, with great attention to detail?
5. Are the colours generally muted and harmonious?

Susie Cooper (1902–95)
From 1922 to 1929, Susie
Cooper worked for A. E. Gray
(see p.48), decorating a variety of
wares in floral, abstract or, more

rarely, geometric hand-painted
designs. These early designs
for Gray's may feature both the
Gray Galleon mark and Cooper's
name. In 1929 she set up her
own decorating business, and
designed and produced her own
wares, buying in blanks from
other manufacturers. In 1931,
she moved into the Crown

Works, Burslem, owned by Wood
& Sons (see p.76), who supplied
her with blanks made to her own
designs. She pioneered technical
advances such as lithographic
transfer printing and developed
a distinctive style of decoration.
Her quietly elegant and understated designs, with their blend
of Modernism and practicality,
established her reputation with
the public and critics alike as
one of the leading tableware
designers of the 20thC, whose
early work in particular is
keenly collected.

Decoration
Early decoration was hand-
painted and favoured decorative
Modernism and stylized
abstraction, as seen on the
Cubist teawares shown above.
* The Cubist pattern is a good
example of Cooper's early
geometric Art Deco designs.
It was also produced in yellow,

beige, and black on tea and coffee wares and in vibrant primary colours on a range of different shapes that included chamber sticks.
* The precise attention to detail in her designs made them equally suitable for hand-painting and lithography.
* From the mid-1930s Susie Cooper pioneered the use of transfer litho-printing at a time when most firms were barely considering the new process of mechanical decoration.
* Popular litho-decoration floral patterns included Dresden Spray (available in four colourways – green, yellow, blue, and, most popular, pink), Gardenia, and Patricia Rose (the most popular pattern, available in four colourways).
* Typical patterns for early Gray wares included hand-painted banding and bold stylized flowers (see p.49).
* Simple graphic repeating patterns were often used; the Star motif shown on the coffee ware, made 1939, left p.124, was a favourite, as were polka dots, exclamation marks, and starbursts.
* From the mid-1930s aerographic and *sgraffito* patterns were used alongside hand-painted patterns. The *sgraffito* design shown on the service plate, c.1938, shown above, features a version of the leaping deer that was a Cooper hallmark in the mid-1920s.

During the 1930s Cooper designed a range of highly practical yet attractive table ware designs, in gently rounded forms, where obvious innovation was restricted to spouts, lids, and handles. Most Cooper wares have shape and pattern numbers. Patterns are applied to a variety of earthenware shapes.
* The Kestrel shape was introduced in 1932 and in production until the 1950s.
* Other shapes include Curlew (1932; decorated with the Stars pattern on the coffee set p.124); Wren (1934); Jay (1935); Falcon (1937), and Spiral (1938).

Later wares
After WWII, Cooper worked on designs for china rather than earthenware to produce a range of lighter, less robust-looking tablewares.
* Many popular patterns were adapted for bone china, with floral designs becoming more abstract in the early 1960s.
* New china shapes included Quail.
* New patterns in clear, modern colours were designed to show off the white porcelain body.
* The Black Fruit breakfast cups below, with polychrome interiors and black print, are a good example of these new trends. This pattern was also used on straight-sided coffee cans.
* Following the take-over by Wedgwood in 1966, many later Susie Cooper designs have Wedgwood marks.

Collecting
* In general, the earlier hand-painted or litho-decorated earthenware ranges are more keenly collected than the later post-war china.
* Specialist reference books (see p.185) will help collectors distinguish between pre- and post-war designs, as many 1920s and '30s designs have been reproduced.
* Hand-painted and litho-decorated wares are equally collectable but the decoration must be in perfect condition: scratches, rubbed patches, or restoration will reduce value.

TRUDA ADAMS

*Vase by Truda Adams (later Carter) for Poole Pottery
c.1930; value code D*

Identification checklist for Truda Adams ceramics
1. Is the pattern bright and vibrant?
2. Is it hand-painted in a free style?
3. Is it painted on opaque white tin glaze on a red/brown body?
4. Does it depict bold stylized flowers, or geometric motifs, or a combination of the two?
5. Is it inspired by French Art Deco patterns?
6. Does it cover most of the surface area?

Truda Adams
In the 1920s and early 1930s the artist and designer Truda Adams (Truda Carter from 1931) designed bright and vibrant patterns for Carter, Stabler & Adams (from 1963 Poole Pottery, see p.62). They were applied by hand by a team of skilled paintresses to a range of now highly collectable hand-thrown ornamental earthenware.

Patterns
* Typically patterns were large, bold, and covered most of the body.
* Most patterns were identified by number rather than name.
* Many designs (see above) were inspired by French flat-pattern portfolios. This particular design is an example of British Jazz Age

Modernism at its best.
* Stylized flowers, and combinations of floral and geometric motifs, were typical, as was a subtle colour palette.
* Among her most popular patterns are Persian Deer (see p.63).
* A number of her designs were later adapted for brooches, produced from 1939, and tablewares.

Collecting
* Condition is vital: restoration will reduce value as will visible damage; some crazing is acceptable.
* Pieces, such as the vase above, with a large decorated surface area are most popular.
* Dark grounds are very rare and desirable.

CHARLOTTE RHEAD

Persian Rose vase by Charlotte Rhead for Crown Ducal
c.1936; value code H

Identification checklist for Charlotte Rhead ceramics
1. Is the piece made of earthenware?
2. Is it hand-painted in a distinctive all-over bold floral or geometric pattern?
3. Does it have tube-lined decoration?
4. Does it show the influence of the Arts and Crafts Movement and Art Deco?
5. Is it marked with a signature?

Charlotte Rhead (1885–1947)
Daughter of Frederick Rhead and sister of Frederick Hurten Rhead, Charlotte was born into a family of talented designers and was trained in a variety of techniques, including tube-lining, enamelling, and *pâte-sur-pâte* from an early age. She worked with her father at Wood & Sons for 14 years, where she became art director in 1912 and built a reputation as a prolific and accomplished designer, before moving to Burgess & Leigh from 1926 to 1931 (see p.55), and then to A. G. Richardson & Co., for whom she created many of her most popular and collectable designs for the Crown Ducal range.

Crown Ducal
From 1931–1942 Rhead worked for Crown Ducal designing patterns for a range of ornmental artware that included freehand-painted chargers, vases, and wall plaques, tableware, and nursery ware.
* The large and varied number of designs included popular floral patterns such as Byzantine (a stylized pattern in oranges and browns that was applied to a variety of forms), Persian Rose, shown above and produced in a variety of colourways, Wisteria and Foxglove.
* Many Crown Ducal patterns had a well-balanced blue and purple palette and a strongly drawn tube-lined pattern.

Marks
* Some early pieces have a tube-lined C. Rhead signature, whereas later pieces have a transfer mark of her full signature. Rhead's tube-lined and trellis patterns for Ellgreave Pottery (est.1921 by Wood & Sons) were sold, and marked, as Lottie Rhead Ware.

127

JESSIE TAIT

Caribbean pattern tableware designed by Jessie Tait for Midwinter mid-1950s; value code H

Identification checklist for Jessie Tait designs
1. Is the pattern semi-abstract or stylized?
2. Is it influenced by contemporary styles in textiles?
3. Do the colourways reflect the popular colour combinations of the period?
4. Is the design original and well-suited to the form?

Jessie Tait
Born in 1928, Jessie Tait was one of the major designers of the 1950s and '60s, producing dozens of imaginative, mainly abstract patterns, for leading tableware manufacturers. Her considerable reputation is all the more remarkable as she worked only as a full-time "in-house" factory designer. Tait's designs are keenly collected.

Midwinter (see pp.94–7)
As leading in-house designer for Midwinter, Tait's designs contributed to the success of Midwinter Modern shapes.
* 1950s Midwinter patterns reflect the fashion for bright colours, an interest in foreign travel, and the influence of contemporary textiles. Popular examples include Primavera (see p.95), Zambesi (see p.94), Red Domino, and Festival. Zambesi and Domino were widely copied by other factories.
* 1960s Midwinter patterns were designed for cylindrical shapes, such as the Fine range, in newly fashionable combinations of blue and green (Spanish Garden, see coffee pot above right) and brown and orange (Sienna, see p.96).

* Tait designed both shape and decoration for a quite rare range of vases, candlesticks, and lemonade sets made from 1956, now highly sought after. Decor-

ation included slip trailing or tube-lining in black, with contemporary-style textures or motifs. Pieces decorated with red or black banding are especially popular.

J. & G. Meakin (see p.13)
After Midwinter's takeover by Meakin in 1968, Tait created successful designs for their new Studio range.
* Popular 1960s patterns include Manderley, Impact, and Inca.

ERIC RAVILIOUS

Edward VIII Coronation mug by
Eric Ravilious 1936; value code F

Identification checklist for Ravilious ceramics
1. Is the piece made by Wedgwood?
2. Is the decoration graphic and highly detailed?
3. Is it perfectly suited to the shape?
4. Is the decoration printed by lithography with hand-painted details?

Eric Ravilious (1903–42)
A talented watercolourist, wood engraver, and illustrator, Ravilious worked as a freelance designer for Josiah Wedgwood & Sons from 1936 until 1942, when he was killed while working as a war artist with the RAF. At Wedgwood Ravilious applied modern design to the company's high-quality traditional tableware lines, reviving the use of on-glaze printing and moving the company towards modern lithographic decoration techniques. Many of his designs were drawn and engraved in the 1930s although not produced until the 1950s owing to wartime restrictions. The originality, charm, and technical skill of his decoration make him one of the most keenly collected 20thC designers.

Designs
Ravilious produced patterns for Wedgwood commemorative ware, such as the Coronation mug above, dinnerware, teaware, and nursery ware.
* Notable tableware patterns include Travel (designed 1938, produced 1953), printed in black on Windsor grey Queens Ware and hand-painted, featuring different types of travel – in particular trains and different types of boat – as the central motif.
* Garden featured a wealth of different central illustrations with a common border and either a graduated yellow band or (rarer) blue band. Small items such as coffee cans and tea cups that just incorporate the border design are more modestly priced. Rarer pieces, such as the large meat plate, with a central illustration of a swimming pool, are expensive.
* Persephone, with a central motif of fish and cornucopias, is the most readily found pattern. Launched as Harvest Festival (1936), it was renamed in 1938 and reintroduced as Coronation Golden Persephone in 1952. It was produced with various coloured bandings and in black on white, which may be of seconds quality and therefore less expensive.
* Other important designs are the Boat Race Day bowl, cup and stand, Afternoon Tea teaware, and Noël Christmas set.

NORTH AMERICAN CERAMICS

Although many major American commercial potteries were only established in the last quarter of the 19thC, by the early 20thC they were expanding rapidly and making a mixture of wares for large and small markets. For the most part they made sturdy utilitarian wares such as stoneware jugs, jars, red clay flower pots, and drainage pipes, as well as mid-range tablewares to meet the demand for stylish but inexpensive wares in china shops and department stores. These serviceable tablewares were made of white earthenware known as semi-vitreous or semi-porcelain; fully vitreous ware was made to supply the huge institutional market with dinner and toilet sets. While the prestigious Lenox company was making top-quality china tableware to order, many other companies produced transfer-decorated white earthenware domestic ranges that sold in huge quantities through dime stores, mail order, and catalogues.

After WWI many factories streamlined their operations and moved to mass-production to cater for market needs. Manufacturers appealed to the huge American home market by producing wares with specifically American names and transfer-printed decoration that featured Native American Indians, Mexican motifs, and indigenous flowers and produce. In the 1930s the California pottery J. A. Bauer launched a range of brightly coloured casual dinnerware, which was very well-suited to the outdoor living and informal entertaining that inspired Fiesta Ware by Frederick Hurten Rhead, and Russel Wright's American Modern (1939–59). This type of solid colour casual mix-and-match dinnerware was designed in the 1930s, and determined the style that was to remain popular for two decades, and influence manufacturers in Europe in the 1950s. Freelance designers played an important part in helping potteries such as Red Wing, Pfaltzgraff, and Hall China Co. to make the transition from utilitarian wares to the new popular casual tableware. Special decorative kitchen items also became an important range as family life, domesticity, and home entertaining became major preoccupations in the early post-war years.

American manufacturers continued to produce ceramics throughout WWII, although fuel and materials were rationed, and many potteries survived by developing products to help the war effort. Post-WWII US potteries producing domestic tablewares faced increasing competition from East Asian manufacturers; some survived by cutting the workforce or increasing mechanized production and switching to institutional wares. However, others were forced to close. In the latter part of the 20thC US institutional wares have been challenged by Chinese products, and American fine-china wares have been challenged by similar products in Europe and Japan.

J. A. BAUER POTTERY CO.

Ring dinnerware by J. A. Bauer
c.1931; value code I

Identification checklist for Bauer Ring tableware
1. Is it made of earthenware or stoneware?
2. Is it thickly potted?
3. Is the form simple and sturdy, with distinctive horizontal ridges or rings?
4. Does it have a brightly coloured monochrome glaze?
5. Is it marked?

J. A. Bauer Pottery Co.
Established in Los Angeles, California, in 1909, Bauer's first products were utilitarian earthenwares and stonewares. By 1916, the modeller and t urner Louis Ipsen had joined the company and production included award-winning art pottery. But Bauer's major success was the launch in the 1930s of a highly influential range of experimental tableware in simple shapes and solid colours that introduced a new casual dining style.

Tablewares
In 1929 Bauer hired Victor Houser to improve the company's colour formulas and glaze quality. These new bright colours, which included black, burgundy, orange-red, chartreuse, Chinese yellow, dark and light blue, grey, ivory, jade green, olive green, light brown, red brown, turquoise, and white, were used on the first American range of casual dinnerware.

* Popular ranges include Ring (c.1931, shown in the main picture and below); Monterey (1936–45; probably designed by Ipsen); and La Linda (1939–59).
* Oil jars (known as ollas) are extremely desirable.
* The simple shapes and solid colours of Bauer's ranges inspired similar ranges by other manufacturers such as Steubenville's highly successful American Modern (see p.168), Homer Laughlin's Fiesta Ware (see p.136), and tableware by Gladding-McBean (see p.146).

WELLER POTTERY

Hudson vase by Weller
c.1915; value code G

Identification checklist for Weller artware
1. Is it made of earthenware?
2. Is it hand-painted in coloured slips?
3. Is it marked?
4. Is the inspiration often historical, or naturalistic?

Weller Pottery
Founded in 1872 by Samuel A. Weller in Fultonham, Ohio, by 1900 the pottery was making a successful range of mid-range artware for florists and giftshops across the US. Weller, a competitive and enterprising businessman, employed craftsmen of many different nationalities, which may have contributed to the successful introduction of so many different ranges. By 1915 Weller claimed to be the largest existing art pottery, but post-WWI, following changes in market demand and the need to streamline production, the company moved towards more industrial, less labour-intensive wares, finally closing in 1948.

Artwares
Many of Weller's early artwares were medium-quality ranges

created to compete with successful lines produced by other manufacturers.
* Louwelsa, with moulded forms with hand-painted underglaze, slip-relief decoration, and a brown overglaze, replicated

Rookwood's Standard Glaze and Roseville's Royal Dark.
* Eocea, with floral slip-relief decoration and a clear overglaze, replicated Rookwood's Iris and Roseville's Royal Light.
* Louwelsa's success spawned

new earthenware art pottery lines decorated with coloured slips.
* Dickensware, introduced 1900, featured hand-painted characters and scenes from Charles Dickens' stories. It also included Native American Indians, as shown on the mug below, c.1900, animals, golfers, and monks.
* The hand-painted Sicardo range, some of which was also embossed, had a distinctive

iridescent glaze, created by the French potter Jacques Sicard, who took the formula with him when he left Weller in 1907.
* Other popular lines include Aurelian, Auroral, Turado, Etna, Floretta, Jap-Birdimal (a tube-line decorated range designed by Frederick Rhead), Dresden, Etched Matt, and Hunter.
* The Soueva line was inspired by Native American Indian pottery and may have been created to compete with Clifton Pottery's Indian Ware. The vase seen bottom p.132, made in 1909, has the characteristic redware body boldly decorated with cream-coloured and black slips.

Post-WWI artwares
In 1920 Weller bought the Zanesville Art Pottery, and employed John Lessell as art director. Lessell designed the last labour-intensive artist-decorated artware lines that Weller produced, including Lamar (dark trees on a red ground), and Lasa, decorated with black landscapes on a lustre ground, as seen on the Lasa vase right, made in the early 1920s.

Production wares
After WWI, Weller focused increasingly on production

wares: vases, jardinières, teaware, planters, lamp bases, and flower bowls were moulded in low relief and then glazed to highlight the featured motif.
* The design was embossed in the mould and colours were added by a hand-painter.
* There was a great variety of motifs. Arcola (1920s) had grapes, vines, or roses in relief with matt glaze; Ardsley (1928) featured cat-tails and water-lilies; Blue Drapery (c.1920) is moulded as dark-blue matt vertical drapery with red roses; Forest (c.1920) is moulded and hand-coloured to look like a forest scene; Chase (c.1940) mimics Wedgwood's jasper ware, with relief hunt scenes in white on a dark-blue matt ground.
* Among the most popular production lines with collectors are Coppertone (1920s), with vases moulded with fish, frogs, and water plants, Muskota, Selma, and Woodcraft.

Collecting and marks
* Collectors expect moulded production pieces to be in perfect condition. Designs featuring animals and creatures are always popular.
* Well-glazed artware pieces command a premium.
* Different trade names were used.
* Various marks were used: all incorporate Weller or Weller Pottery, and some included the line name as well.

COWAN POTTERY

Lustre vases by Cowan
late 1920s; value code H

Identification checklist for Cowan vases
1. Is it made of porcelain?
2. Does it have a white body?
3. Is the form inspired by Oriental ceramics but with contemporary styling?
4. Does it have a brilliant glaze in a modern colour?
5. Is it marked?

Cowan Pottery
Founded in 1912 by Reginald Guy Cowan, a teacher of ceramics and design, the pottery closed when he joined the army in 1917 and reopened in 1919, relocating the following year to Rocky River, Ohio. Here he was joined by a group of young artists who designed sculpture and artware, and the early redware pieces were replaced by high-fired porcelain wares, including slip-cast statuettes. The pottery closed in 1931 when Cowan became art director of Onondaga Pottery (see p.160).

Wares
* Most Cowan Pottery was mass-produced and widely distributed.
* The "studio" lines created by independent designers and often issued in limited editions are highly collectable. They were generally made after 1927.
* The exceptional variety of glazes included matt, glossy, and lustre finishes.

Marks
* Early ware has an impressed or printed Cowan Pottery mark.

* Pieces designed by Cowan himself are typically marked with a relief-moulded Cowan, sometimes with an R G monogram below.
* A range of inexpensive flower vases was made for retail florists between 1927 and 1931; some of these wares have an impressed Lakeside mark.

JUGTOWN POTTERY

Vase by Jugtown
c.1930; value code H

Identification checklist for Jugtown wares
1. Is it hand-thrown?
2. Is it made of stoneware?
3. Is the shape perhaps influenced by a combination of traditional Korean and Chinese ceramics?
4. Or is the piece a traditional North Carolina pottery form?
5. Does it have a distinctive glaze?
6. Is it marked?

Jugtown Pottery
Founded in 1921 in Jugtown, North Carolina, by Jacques and Juliana Busbee, the pottery, which is still active but under different ownership, produced custom giftware, dinnerware, traditional North Carolina stoneware, and bright-orange earthenware. Jacques Busbee also devised a hybrid style, which combined traditional Chinese and Korean shapes with distinctive glazes, as seen in the vase reminiscent of Chinese bronzes as seen above.

Wares
Production concentrated on red earthenware, stoneware, dinnerware, and artware.
* These hybrid pieces, which included dishes and vases, were made in native stoneware and decorated with various glazes: thick white, mirror black, a greenish "frogskin" of salt glaze over Albany slip, and a transmutational red/turquoise called Chinese Blue, seen on the vase above.
* Traditional redware bodies were glazed to give a pumpkin-orange colour.
* After 1971, bodies and glazes were reformulated to meet regulations prohibiting the use of low-fired lead glazes on food ware.

Marks
* An impressed circular stamp featuring an outline of a jug and the words JUGTOWN WARE.
* From 1960 until 1977, the jug is sometimes replaced by a pitcher. * After 1977, a date is sometimes included.

HOMER LAUGHLIN CHINA

Fiesta Ware by Frederick H. Rhead for Homer Laughlin
1930s and 1940s; value code I

Identification checklist for Fiesta Ware
1. Are the forms rounded?
2. Do they have distinctive ridged detailing
   on rims, feet, lids, handles, and flatware borders?
3. Are the serving items decorated with
   concentric circles?
4. Are they made in bright solid colours?
5. Are they marked on the base?

Homer Laughlin China Co.
(est. 1877; still active)
Founded in East Liverpool,
Ohio, and incorporated as
Homer Laughlin China
Company in 1896, it developed
rapidly due to its emphasis on
market demands combined with
excellent business sense. By
1902 it had three factories and
in 1905 it created its own village
and factory complex across the
River Oio in Newell, West
Virginia. By 1912 the company's
110 kilns were suppling 10 per
cent of the US ceramics market.

Wares
Tableware and kitchenware was
produced at modest prices
and to suit every taste from
traditional to modern. The
China Book catalogue below left,
issued in 1912, shows Pattern
H-135, which is typical of the
semi-vitreous ware made in
the traditional style of French
Limoges china, with fancy
shapes and decorated with
tiny flowers.
* In 1925–26 the company
developed an ivory earthenware
body called Yellowstone
following Lenox's success with
fine china in the early 1920s
(see p.139).
* Litho decoration predominated,
and several solid-colour modern
ranges were also issued with
litho decoration on an ivory body.
* Floral patterns were particularly
popular in the American market
in the 1920s and 1930s. The
Tulips in a Basket pattern seen
on the plate, cup, and saucer
illustrated on p.137 is just one
example of the company's large
range of successful floral litho
decoration.

Important designers

The two best-known designers of the many who worked in the company's design and modelling departments over the years are probably Frederick Hurten Rhead and Don Schreckengost, who created the company's popular and successful modern ranges that are now eagerly collected.

* Rhead, art director from 1927, created Fiesta Ware (1936–72; revived 1986), see main picture, the most popular solid-colour casual dinnerware made in the US.
* Available in a bright range of colours to mix and match, Fiesta was mass-produced from the late 1930s throughout the 1950s. Some Fiesta pieces are still in production today; modern versions have lighter colours

than the originals.
* Fiesta is the most collectable and prolific range. It is still accessible and there are many rarities such as unusual shape/colour combinations.
* Other popular Rhead designs include Century, a square shape introduced in 1931 with an ivory body and litho patterns such as Mexicana, Hacienda, Conchita, and English Garden. In 1937 it was issued with solid brightly coloured glazes as Riviera.
* The Wells shape, designed by Rhead, was introduced in 1930

with a range of semi-matt art glazes in blue, leaf green, peach, rust brown, melon yellow, and a vellum ivory that was sometimes decorated with litho.
* Rhead's Kitchen Kraft OvenServe line (1937) was also decorated with solid Fiesta colours and litho on ivory.
* Schreckengost contributed Jubilee Ware, shown below, issued in 1948 to celebrate the company's 75th anniversary. Originally decorated in solid pastel colour glazes, in 1952 the same shape was issued with white handles in brown (Suntone) and blue (Skytone).
* Other popular Schreckengost designs include Epicure (1953) and Rhythm (1955), a slim coupé shape in solid colours or with decal patterns such as Golden Wheat (wheat was a popular motif used on American dinnerware in the 1940s and '50s).

Marks

Since 1900, dinnerware backstamps have date codes included that identify the year each piece was made.
* 1900–09: single-digit month and single-digit year followed by 1, 2, or 3 to show factory of origin.
* 1910–20: first numeral identifies month, next two numerals year, and letter and/or digit cluster the factory of origin.
* 1921–29: letter identifies month, single digit the year, last figure the factory of origin.
* 1930–60: letter identifies month, two digits the year, letter and number combination the factory of origin.
* 1960– : discrete combination of two letters identifies month and year (eg May 1965 is FE).
* Homer Laughlin backstamps are specific to ware and pattern and include the company name and/or the H L cipher.

LENOX

Silver-overlay dessert pieces by Lenox
1920; value codes H/I

Identification checklist for Lenox dinnerwares
1. Is it made of bone china?
2. Is the china ivory-coloured?
3. Is it exquisitely decorated, either with enamelling or gilding, or perhaps silver overlay?
4. Are the pattern and shape traditional?
5. Is it marked?

Lenox

Walter Lenox founded the Ceramic Art Company in 1899 in Trenton, New Jersey, to make artware. In 1906, the company changed both its name (to Lenox) and major direction following the success of its dinnerware range, on which its reputation was largely built. After 1950, as production expanded, Lenox acquired a new factory in Pomona, New Jersey, broadened its market with more affordable dinnerwares and continued with its successful range of giftware.

Artware

Lenox's finely crafted ivory china was hand-painted by the leading decorators in the US, some of whom were European immigrants. All specialized in a different type of subject.
* The English uncle and nephew William and George Morley specialized in flower painting. William also produced masterly fruit, fish, and game sets. The Orchid plate above is

from a 1926 set of 12 plates decorated with orchids, each plate showing a different species as the central motif.
* Hans Nosek (Bohemian) painted putti and beautiful women; Sigmund Wirkner (German) painted figures.
* The American decorator Kate Sears used a penknife to carve greenware (unfired clay) into elaborate figural scenes.
* These earliest hand-painted artwares and cabinet plates are the most expensive Lenox collectables.

Dinnerware

A new white bone-china formula for dinnerware was developed c.1900, and by 1906 the successful new dinnerware lines dominated production. The white bone china was fully replaced by Lenox's characteristic ivory-coloured china in 1920.

* The earliest services were individually designed and decorated with enamelling and gilding by the highly skilled artware decorators (see bottom p.9). Such highly expensive made-to-order sets are rarely available to collectors.

* From c.1910 stock patterns were added, often printed and filled patterns or decalcomania.

* Lenox china blanks were also decorated with silver overlay by silver manufacturers, such as the Rockwell Silver Co., who probably decorated the service in the main picture. Silver-overlay vases and tea sets can be found today.

* Frank Graham Holmes, chief designer from 1906 until 1954, created many popular patterns from historical styles to Art Deco. His traditional patterns such as Autumn (1919–present) and Ming (1917–66) have been enduringly popular.

* In 1917 President and Mrs Woodrow Wilson commissioned china for the White House. Commissions from heads of state around the world followed, and Lenox china was made for America's first families through-out the 1920s, '30s and '40s, and for President and Mrs Reagan in 1984.

Giftware

In general, Lenox's giftware is more collectable than the company's dinnerware. Lenox's ivory body could be stained several colours, including salmon-pink, yellow, sage green, and medium blue. Contrasting coloured bodies were used on a new variety of giftware (and dinnerware) from the 1930s to the 1950s, as shown on the salmon-pink and ivory cachepots and bird figure above (c.1940).

* Art Deco figurines, streamlined vases and boudoir lamps are very sought after.

* Patricia Eakin figurines are another popular collecting niche. The range, made in the 1940s and early 1950s, exploited the versatility of Lenox's strong yet delicate ivory body and includes Mistress Mary, Floradora, Colonial Lady, Natchez Belle, and the Ballerina, shown below.

* The figurines were meticulously assembled from slip-cast and handmade parts. Ruffles, ribbons, and bows, such as the Ballerina's tutu, were moulded, rolled, folded, and draped by hand. This process is not uncommon, with good-quality figures, and was used on ranges like Doulton's flower-sellers (see p.83).

RED WING POTTERIES

Magnolia pattern dinnerware by Red Wing 1940s; value code I

Identification checklist for Red Wing dinnerwares
1. Is the body earthenware?
2. Does it have a rounded and curving, often asymmetrical and modern shape?
3. Does it have a hand-painted contemporary pattern?
4. Or is it a solid modern colour?
5. Is it marked?

Red Wing Potteries Inc.
Established in Red Wing, Minnesota, in 1877, the pottery produced utilitarian stonewares until the early 1930s, when it began to produce artwares, and, from 1935, dinnerwares. In 1936 the company's name was changed to Red Wing Potteries

Inc., and stoneware production ceased in 1947. Red Wing commissioned artware and dinnerware from a number of distinguished designers and enjoyed considerable market success from the 1940s until the 1960s, closing in 1967.

Early artwares
The new Red Wing ranges included florists' crockery and artware made from 1933 until 1938 for George Rumrill. Typical shapes included vases, candlesticks, bowls, ashtrays, candy dishes, book-ends, planters, and garden crockery.
* RumRill shapes, though often based on traditional forms, generally followed 1930s styles, with softened contours and simplified design elements, as shown on the RumRill vase left, made in the 1930s.
* A variety of pastel matt glazes were used.
* Commonly used motifs were

leaf forms, nudes, cornucopias, swans and other birds, fruits, shells, and flowers.

Dinnerware

The success of the first dinnerware line, introduced in 1935, was followed by a number of innovative and stylish modern ranges by well-known designers that reflected the move towards informal entertaining.

* In 1939 Belle Kogan designed the Gypsy Trail Hostess Ware, issued in four different styles: Plain; Chevron – plain, brightly

coloured, with animal handles; Fondoso – bright or pastel colours, with low-relief geometric patterns; and Reed – with vertical ribbing.

* The Town and Country range, designed by Eva Zeisel (see p.167) in 1946 and launched in 1947, was a groundbreaking biomorphic design, with slightly asymmetrical shapes, and glossy and semi-matt glazes.

Charles Murphy

The designer Charles Murphy joined Red Wing in 1940, and in the late 1940s he reorganized the decorators into a mass-production assembly unit, with each worker painting part of a pattern rather than the whole.

He designed both artware and dinnerware, and, from 1953 when he became design consultant, produced over 70 hand-painted dinnerware patterns, creating a large number of Red Wing's most popular patterns.

* His early dinnerwares such as Brittany and Orleans featured hand-painted designs. The Magnolia pattern, shown in the main picture on the Concord shape, is typically painted in a bold, freehand style but uses a quiet 1940s palette.

* The popular Capistrano and Tampico patterns, introduced 1955, won critical acclaim. Brightly painted and exotic, they captured the post-war desire for colour and exciting foreign travel.

* Other quintessential elements of 1950s style – bright colours, asymmetry, and overlapping graphic free-form motifs – can be seen on the plate (left) designed by Murphy in the 1950s.

* His most commercially successful pattern was the Bob White bird-inspired line on the Casual shape, introduced in 1955 in a wide variety of kitchenware forms.

* The Bob White casserole and bird-shaped hors d'oeuvre holder (with holes in its back for toothpicks), shown below, are special pieces, although other items from the range are more valuable.

* Murphy artwares for Red Wing included a short-lived range of high-priced modelled figures, introduced in 1942, and several hundred art pottery shapes designed throughout his tenure. Among the most popular today are *Sgraffito*, Hobnail, Decorator Line, Chromoline, and Doric Ensemble.

HALL CHINA COMPANY

*Refrigerator ware by Hall China
1940s; value codes H/I*

Identification checklist for Hall's Moderne refrigerator ware

1. Does it have a moulded streamlined form?
2. Does it have a bright solid colour?
3. Is it a piece of functional kitchenware?
4. Is it made of stoneware?
5. Is it marked? (see below)

Hall China Company

Established in East Liverpool, Ohio, in 1903, Hall's production and sales only began to grow after Robert T. Hall, son of the founder, developed a high-temperature leadless glaze that allowed the firm to make one-fire ware with a non-crazing glaze. During WWI, Hall supplied the kitchenware for restaurants and institutions that had previously been supplied by European manufacturers. It retained the market because of the superior quality of its wares, and, in the interwar years, streamlined shapes and new brilliant colours. Teapots, kitchenware, dinnerware, and consumer premiums remain staple products, and the huge range of shapes and patterns offers collectors an exceptionally wide choice.

Teapots

By 1920 the teapot line had expanded greatly through new production techniques and advertising campaigns on the proper way to brew tea, and Hall claimed to be the world's largest manufacturer of decorated teapots.
* By the end of the 20thC Hall

had produced over 2,000 teapot designs using different combinations of shape, size, colour, and decoration.
* The 1930s Aladdin teapot below, for example, came in 21 different colours, including black, pink, pale yellow, three different greens, three different

cobalt blues, two different browns, orchid, rose, ivory, warm yellow, and Chinese Red – one of the most popular colours for Hall's kitchenware.
* The Aladdin teapot with the lithographic transfer Crocus pattern is one of the most popular Crocus pieces.

Consumer premiums

The lithographic transfers added to the wares from 1931 opened new markets for premiums (free gifts) and dinnerware. The first premiums were made for tea and

142

coffee companies such as Best Tea, Cook Coffee, Great American Tea, Standard Coffee, the Grand Union Company, and the Jewel Tea Company.

* The Red Poppy pattern for Grand Union, and the Wildfire premium range with a white body made for the Great American Tea Company, are favourites with collectors.

* The Autumn Leaf pattern, made for Jewel Tea from 1933 to 1938, is another favourite, with its own collectors' club. The pattern is found on a wide variety of kitchenware, such as the Autumn nesting bowls, shown right, made in the 1940s.

* Butter dishes, clocks, the Jordan drip coffee pot, and the single-handed New England bean pot are the most expensive Hall Autumn Leaf pieces.

* Tea and coffee companies frequently switched manufacturers so the same litho patterns are found on ranges by other firms. Hall versions seem to be the most collectable.

Another popular collecting area is the premiums given away with the new electric refrigerators produced from c.1940. Hall produced butter dishes, leftover containers, water servers (as shown in the main picture), casseroles and bowls in streamlined shapes and brilliant colours for many manufacturers.

* The streamlined designs and bright colours are now popular with collectors.

* Water servers are the most valuable refrigerator premiums because of their large size and lids.

* The water servers made for Aristocrat and Sears are always particularly popular with collectors.

Dinnerware
American economic expansion after WWII encouraged Hall to develop its dinnerware range by commissioning new patterns and shapes from freelance designers. The English designer J. Palin Thorley designed Granitone, a traditional Neo-classical patte rn decorated with printed floral patterns, and the Hungarian-born designer Eva Zeisel (see p.166) created two particularly distinctive modern ranges for Hall.

* In 1954 Zeisel also designed

refrigerator jars, now very collectable (see p.167), as part of Tomorrow's Classic 20-piece overproof cookware and kitchen accessories range.

* Tomorrow's Classic was designed in 1949–50 and produced from 1952. Its organic shapes and cheerful decoration made it the most popular of Zeisel's dinnerware ranges.

* Century (1956; see pp.166–67),

made in white, had a graceful but fragile tear-drop shape that stacked and nested well and was enhanced by delicate graphic printed patterns.

Collecting
* Kitchenware and serving ware: Blue Blossom and Blue Garden (both 1939).
* Patterns: Floral: Meadow Flower, Poppy, Poppy and Wheat, Red Poppy and Rose Parade; Taverne Silhouette.
* Premiums: water servers – Phoenix, Hercules, Nova. Matching lids are essential for maximum value.

Marks
* All marks include Hall or Hall's.
* The word KITCHENWARE (see below) was added from 1932.
* Hallcraft pieces designed by Eva Zeisel have a litho-printed facsimile signature mark.

W. S. GEORGE POTTERY

Striped platter by W. S. George 1954; value code 1

Identification checklist for W. S. George dinnerware
1. Is the body china or semi-porcelain?
2. Is it a piece of dinnerware?
3. Does it have a white or creamy yellow body?
4. Does it have printed decoration?
5. Is it marked?

W. S. George Pottery
Founded in 1904 in East Palestine, Ohio, the pottery made china and semi-porcelain dinnerware in a wide variety of shapes and decoration for sale in department stores and "five and dime" stores that sold inexpensive goods. From 1925, the firm was managed by W. C. George, son of the founder, who greatly improved production methods and equipment. The pottery closed in 1960.

Tablewares
The many different shapes and patterns (both stylish, as seen in the main picture, or traditional) offer collectors a wide variety of combinations. Patterns were offered on Canarytone – a creamy yellow glaze inspired by the success of Lenox's ivory body (see p.139) – or white.
* Favourite collecting shapes include Rainbow, Georgette (sometimes called Petal), Ranchero, and Lido.
* The Lido shape, shown on the hand-painted 1930s Tulip plate right, was launched in 1932

and made in both white and Canarytone.
* Popular patterns used on the Ranchero shape include Wheat, Wampum, Iroquois Red, Indian Corn, and Fruit Fantasy.
* Popular patterns applied to Lido include Blossoms, Mexi-Lido, Mexi-Gren, Plain Jane, and Flower Rim.

* W. S. George pottery is readily found in a wide variety of shapes and patterns.
* Marks usually incorporate the product line, shape line, and company name.

VERNON KILNS

Hey Day pattern dinnerware by Vernon Kilns
late 1940s; value code I

Identification checklist for Vernon Kilns' dinnerware
1. Is it made of earthenware?
2. Does it have a modern shape?
3. Is it decorated with a low-relief pattern and pastel glazes?
4. Or, alternatively, is it decorated in solid colours and contemporary printed decoration?
5. Is it marked?

Vernon Kilns
Established in Los Angeles, California, in 1931, Vernon Kilns' production included dinnerware, decorative plates, figures of film stars, and Walt Disney characters (1941–42), and, from 1947, speciality wares. The pottery closed in 1958, having produced over 1,000 different designs – the largest variety of collectable designs of any Californian pottery.

Wares
From 1936 to the early 1940s Vernon's best-known designs were decorative plates by Rockwell Kent.
* The Moby Dick series (1936), see plate right, was transfer-printed with Kent's illustrations for Herman Melville's book. Designs were issued in Dark Blue, Maroon, Light Orange, and Walnut Brown.
* The Salamina series (1939) was based on Rockwell's account of his life in Greenland.
* From 1936–37, May and

Genevieve Hamilton designed the Rhythmic and Rippled dinnerware patterns, and a range of modern tableware shapes with pastel glazes fashionable in the 1930s.

* Later popular modern dinnerware shapes include Anytime (c.1955), and San Marino (1947), shown in the main picture, in the Hey Day pattern with a typically muted colourway.
* Popular patterns today include Tickled Pink, Heavenly Days, and Imperial.

145

GLADDING-MCBEAN

Franciscan Apple dinnerware by Gladding-McBean
1940s; value code I

Identification checklist for Franciscan dinnerware
1. Is it made of cream-coloured earthenware?
2. Does it have moulded low-relief decoration?
3. Does it have hand-painted underglaze decoration?
4. Does it have an informal decorative style?
5. Is it without gold or platinum decoration?
6. Is it marked? (see right)

Gladding-McBean
Established in 1875 in Los Angeles, California, by 1926 the company was the largest manufacturer of utilitarian clay products in the US. From the 1930s to the 1970s, a highly successful range of dinnerwares was also produced, together with artware and dinnerware ranges using the designs and moulds acquired during the takeover in 1937 of Catalina Clay Products.

Early Franciscan Ware
The Franciscan Ware gift and tableware range, designed by Mary K. Grant, was introduced in 1934. The earthenware body was durable, virtually without crazing and designed for a one-

fire process, which reduced production costs.
* It had low-relief decoration that was hand-painted with oxide stains in the mould, then fired to give a hand-painted underglaze finish.
* The first tableware pattern, El Patio, like the early coloured bowl shown left, made in the 1930s, was influenced by J. A. Bauer's new ranges (see p.131), and featured eight bright solid colours.
* Patterns introduced in the mid-late 1930s included Coronado, Avalon, Del Oro, Mango, and Pueblo.
* From the late 1930s a range of fruit and flower patterns were introduced, including Hawthorne, Geranium, Ivy (1948), Apple (1940; shown in the main picture), and Desert Rose (1941). Ivy, Apple, and Desert Rose are classic patterns that have remained perennially popular.
* Desert Rose is probably the most popular pattern ever made: by 1964, there were 60 million pieces.

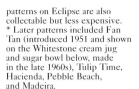

* In 1939 the New York Metropolitan Museum of Art commissioned the Franciscan plant to produce the first square dinnerware made in the USA, designed by Morris B. Sanders. It was renamed Tiempo in 1949.

In 1941 fine china products were added to the Franciscan Ware, and by 1947 the company used Franciscan Fine China and Masterpiece China to differentiate the two china lines.
* The Masterpiece China Line (1941–79) finally included nine basic shapes with 165 patterns designed by Otto J. Lund and George James.

Later Franciscan wares

In 1952 Mary J. Winans succeeded Mary K. Grant as head of the design department. A large staff of designers created many new patterns and a white earthenware – Whitestone Ware – was added to the popular cream-coloured earthenware patterns that had been made since the 1940s.
* The most popular modern Franciscan lithol line is the Eclipse coupé shape decorated with the Starburst pattern (introduced 1954), as shown on the Starburst plate above made in the late 1950s.
* The Duet (introduced 1956) and Oasis (introduced 1955)

patterns on Eclipse are also collectable but less expensive.
* Later patterns included Fan Tan (introduced 1951 and shown on the Whitestone cream jug and sugar bowl below, made in the late 1960s), Tulip Time, Hacienda, Pebble Beach, and Madeira.

In 1962 the Franciscan plant was acquired by the Lock Joint Pipe Company, and Franciscan Ware made under this ownership carries the name Interpace in the mark. Franciscan Ware was then acquired by Wedgwood in 1979, and in 1984 manufacturing of the remaining Franciscan Ware patterns transferred to England, where they are now made by Johnson Bros.

Other wares

In 1937 Gladding-McBean acquired Catalina Clay Products and produced artware and dinnerware using Catalina designs and moulds until 1942.
* Catalina Rancho, a solid-colour casual dinnerware, was popular between 1937 and 1941.
* Popular artwares included figures and flower holders in an ox-blood glaze on Chinese-style shapes.
* Other Catalina art and tablewares had colourful monochrome and duotone glazes featuring blue, gold, agate, and green.

IROQUOIS CHINA COMPANY

Impromptu shape teaware with Jardinières pattern by Iroquois late 1950s; value code I

Identification checklist for Impromptu tablewares
1. Does it have an unusual stylish modern shape?
2. Does it have distinctive handles and knobs?
3. Is it made of vitreous china?
4. Does it have contemporary transfer-printed decoration, perhaps floral or geometric, naturalistic or stylized?
5. Is it marked?

Iroquois China Company
Established in 1905 in Syracuse, New York, the company's early hotel wares were unremarkable. In 1946, Russel Wright (see pp.168–69) designed the Casual China range for Iroquois, which, together with the other general market tableware designed by Ben Seibel, remained Iroquois's most successful products until the company closed in 1969.

Tablewares
Iroquois's high-fired vitreous china body was sturdy and suited both to the newly fashionable informal tableware ranges and oven-to-table wares.
* Russel Wright's Casual China range was launched in 1946. After early teething problems with the glaze and body were solved, the range broke its own sale records for ten years.
* Casual's smooth modern style was developed from the coupé shape, and the recessed handles were designed to be moulded into the body.
* In 1951 the handles were redesigned as knobs but the earlier-style recessed handles continued to be made.
* Casual China was made

in a range of solid colours, including Sugar White, Lemon Yellow, Ice Blue, Nutmeg, Avocado Yellow, Parsley Green, Oyster, Charcoal, Ripe Apricot, Pink Sherbet, Lettuce Green, Canteloupe, Aqua, and Brick.
* Ben Seibel's ranges of tableware included Interplay (1954, now rare); Impromptu (1956); Informal, Inheritance, and Intaglio.
* Inheritance and Intaglio are difficult to find today.
* Impromptu (shown in the main picture with the Jardinières pattern) is relatively easily found and was issued with a variety of patterns – floral, geometric, naturalistic, and stylized.
* Impromptu dinnerware, including a condiment set, was also produced.
* Informal, also easily collected, had transfer-printed patterns with coordinating solid colours on the reverse side. Bowls have the solid colour on the exterior, plates on the bottom, and cups on the inside.
* Informal pieces without transfer-printed decoration have solid colour inside.
* Marks identify the manufacturer, shape line, and designer.

PFALTZGRAFF POTTERY

Artware by Pfaltzgraff
1932–37; value codes H/I

Identification checklist for Pfaltzgraff artwares
1. Is it made of moulded stoneware?
2. Is it a decorative shape?
3. Does it have airbrushed, mottled, or crystalline effects?
4. Is it coloured blue, green, pink, mauve, or pumpkin yellow?
5. Is it marked?

Pfaltzgraff Pottery wares
One of the oldest family-owned potteries in continuous production in the US, the company, still active, was reorganized as Pfaltzgraff Pottery in West York, Pennsylvania, in 1906. Early wares included utilitarian stoneware, flower pots, and florists' items. The artware line of flower containers, seen in the main picture, was made between 1932 and 1937. In the

late 1930s the pottery added cookware and bakeware to production, and from the 1950s, dinnerware, which became a major product during the second-half of the 20thC.
* The first dinner plate shape, made in 1951, was developed from the Gourmet Royale range of giftware.
* Yorktowne, introduced in 1967 and seen on the plate left made in 1969, was the first dinnerware pattern created by the in-house design department set up in the mid-1960s.
* It is probably the pottery's most recognizable pattern and was based on the brushed blue flower decoration typically used on utilitarian stonewares from 1850 to 1875 in the mid-Atlantic region.
* During the late 1970s the Yorktowne, Gourmet, and Heritage dinnerware ranges made up almost 75 per cent of production.

HAEGER POTTERIES

Pierced vase and heart-shaped ashtray by Haeger
1950s; value code I

Identification checklist for Haeger Pottery
1. Is it made of earthenware?
2. Is it brightly coloured?
3. Does it have a decorative or novel form?
4. Does it have a brilliant glaze?
5. Is it marked?

Haeger Potteries
Established in Dundee, Illinois, in 1871, Haeger made giftware from 1914 and dinnerware from 1919. The Royal Haeger artware

line, named after its designer Royal Ardman Hickman, was introduced in 1938, and its highly successful range of vases, figurines, and flower containers, such as the decorative double-shell cornucopia planter (c1940)

below, are keenly collected today. In the 1950s the Royal Haeger line included ornaments, lamps, and novelties, such as the fish-shaped jug vase shown left and planter below, in shapes inspired by figures, animals, and abstract forms interpreted in a populist style.
* Hickman's stalking black panther design was copied by more than 30 other potteries.
* From 1947 until 1972, the European designer Eric Olsen, who had also worked for Spode and Minton, created most of the artware and lamp designs. The Red Bull is one of his best-known designs.

HARKER POTTERY COMPANY

*Engraved platter with Coronet pattern by Harker
1955–60; value code I*

Identification checklist for Harker Ware
1. Is it made of earthenware?
2. Is it dinner, or kitchenware?
3. Does it have a white body?
4. Is it decorated with lithographic transfer patterns?
5. Or does it have a solid-colour top layer cut away
to reveal a white body?
6. Is it marked?

Harker Pottery Company
Founded in 1899, in 1931
the company moved from East
Liverpool, Ohio, to a newer
plant in Chester, West Virginia.
Production concentrated on
mix-and-match transfer-printed
kitchenware and dinnerware.
By 1965 Harker's was producing
over 25 million pieces annually.
The factory closed after fire
damage in 1975.

Cameo and Engraved Ware
The Cameo process, in which
the solid top colour was cut
away to reveal the white body
beneath, was originally used
by George Bauer to create a
Cameoware range for another
pottery. It was sold to Harker,
who paid royalties to Bauer,
and by 1941 was used on kitchen
and dinnerware.
* Dainty Flower and White Rose
are the most commonly found
Cameoware patterns.
* The Kiddo Cameo children's

range included shapes and
patterns based on animals
and children's toys.
* When Cameoware was
discontinued, the Cameo process
was used into the 1950s on the
Engraved range that replaced it.
* Engraved was produced in
a wider range of colours, and
popular patterns included
Country Cousins, Petit Fleur,
Star-lite, and the Coronet pattern
shown above.

Other wares
In 1926 Harker introduced
Hotoven, its first kitchenware
range.
* The range is keenly collected
today.
* The White Clover dinnerware
range (1953–58) was designed
by Russel Wright (see p.169).
* Harker's most popular semi-
vitreous dinnerware was the
Royal Gadroon shape, produced
from 1947 to 1963 with a variety
of printed patterns.

STANGL POTTERY

*Orchard pattern coffee pot by Stangl
1950s; value code I*

Identification checklist for Stangl dinner and tablewares
1. Does it have a redware body?
2. Is it decorated by hand?
3. Does the pattern include *sgrafitto* decoration, perhaps combined with hand-painting?
4. Is the pattern made up of fruit-and-flower motifs?
5. Is it marked?

Stangl Pottery
Founded in association with the Fulper Pottery Company in 1926, the Stangl Pottery name was adopted officially in 1955, although it had been associated with wares made at the Fulper Trenton factory, New Jersey, from the 1930s. Manufacturing ceased in 1978.

Decoration
A variety of different decorative techniques was used on the company's redware bodies.
* The earliest dinnerware ranges, such as Colonial (1932) and Americana, were decorated with solid colours in an informal style.
* Cheerful *sgrafitto*-decorated patterns were used on other early tablewares.
* From the early 1940s, the *sgraffito* decoration was embellished with painted decoration, usually fruit and flowers with strong, colourful borders as seen on the Orchard coffee pot above.
* Fruit-and-flower patterns with neutral background colours and

limited colour ranges were used in the 1950s.

Wares
* From 1940 to 1978 Stangl produced a range of bird figurines designed by Auguste Jacob.
* The huge range of birds, which included ducks, cardinals, blue jays, love-birds, orioles, and roosters, were slip-cast in moulds and hand-painted so that no two were identical.
* The range of Stoby Mugs designed by Toby Sarg was introduced in 1936. These character mugs were made in moulds and then hand-painted. Today they command relatively high prices.
* From 1942 until the 1970s Stangl produced Kiddie Ware or Kiddie Sets, comprising a cup and compartment dish (two-piece set), or plate, cup, and bowl (three-piece set), decorated with motifs from nursery rhymes and stories, including Mother Goose, Humpty Dumpty, and Little Boy Blue.

Cowboy Boots lamp by Nelson McCoy
1950s; value code H

Identification checklist for Nelson McCoy pottery
1. Does it have an imaginative novelty shape?
2. Is it made of moulded earthenware?
3. Is it highly coloured?
4. Is it marked?

Nelson McCoy Pottery
Founded in 1910 in Roseville, Ohio, the company made only stoneware kitchen items until 1926, when a range of industrial moulded artware was introduced. From 1940 until its closure in 1990 McCoy's main product was cookie jars, although it also made a range of outdoor and casual table and serving wares, and figural and decorative flower pots, jardinières, planters, wall pockets, lamp bases, and vases.

Wares
* Cookie jars (see p.161) are the company's best-known and most sought-after pieces.
* Popular and collectable tea sets include Pine Cone (1945), Ivy (1949), Daisy (1953), and Moderne (1954).
* Brown Drip dinnerware was made over a long period and included a wide variety of tableware, teaware, and kitchenware.
* Flower holders, lamp bases, and vases were made in a variety of novel shapes. The cowboy boots used as a lamp base above were also used for vases and planters.
* Other novelty forms included Stretch Animals, Alligator, Banana Boat, Ducks, Humpty Dumpty, Frog with Lotus, or Umbrella, Piano, Pig, Rodeo Cowboy, Uncle Sam, and Scotties.
* The McCoy planter range was large and diverse, with a wide variety of models to create novelty. Popular characters, animals, and sea life were used, as well as motifs more directly related to plants and flowers.

153

*China coffee pot by Knowles, Taylor & Knowles
c.1905; value code I*

**Identification checklist for Knowles, Taylor
& Knowles tableware**
1. Is it made of semi-porcelain?
2. Does it have a traditional shape?
3. Does it perhaps have some moulded detail?
4. Does it perhaps have transfer-printed decoration,
either customized for an institution, or in traditional
floral patterns?
5. Does it have a glossy glaze, perhaps with
an additional spray-on matt finish?
6. Is it marked?

Knowles, Taylor & Knowles
The company, founded in 1870
in East Liverpool, Ohio,
eventually became the largest
manufacturer of dinnerware
in the United States. Its success
was due to increased
mechanization and expanding
markets in the USA. Fine-art
porcelain Belleek Ware was
made from 1889, but production
ceased following a fire in 1890.
The company then made
a bone-china Lotus Ware artware
range until 1897, when
production switched to semi-
porcelain tableware. By 1900
the pottery was producing

institutional ware, hotel ware
and specialities for hospitals
and asylums. Following the
economic depression of the
mid-1920s, the factory closed
in 1931.

Wares

The semi-porcelain tablewares, institutional wares, toilet sets, spittoons, etc, were made

in traditional shapes with traditional decoration.
* Many of the transfer-printed decorations were floral, and many patterns were named after individual states: for example, the overall pattern of small blue rosebuds was known as Virginia.
* Some wares, such as the coffee pot in the main picture, were decorated with moulded details, with a pale-coloured matt finish sprayed over the glossy glaze, and gilded detail.
* Many of the pottery's shapes were named after US colleges, such as Harvard, Yale, Cornell, and Oberlin.

Edwin M. Knowles China Co. (1900–62)

The company was established in Chester, West Virginia, opposite East Liverpool, by Edwin Knowles, son of Isaac Knowles, the founder of Knowles, Taylor & Knowles. Original production included semi-vitreous tableware and toilet ware, spittoons, and Ohio covered jugs. By 1940, the company was the third largest pottery in the United States but succumbed to market change following WWII and closed in 1962.

Wares

The main production was semi-porcelain tableware, including dinner services, serving pieces, and kitchenware.
* Wares were made in both traditional and modern moulded shapes.
* The matching hollowware for the Hostess platter shown bottom p.154, made in the late 1930s, had stylish angular handles and terraced finials.
* Utility Ware – a semi-vitreous kitchenware – was produced from 1939 to the late 1940s. It was decorated both in fashionable solid colours and with brightly coloured bands, and with coloured transfer-printed patterns, such as Valencia, shown on the plate above made in 1943.
* Among the ranges most popular with collectors are Deanna (1938), a solid-colour ware with printed decoration on the ivory version, and Yorktowne (1936), a globular-shaped Art Deco ware with colourful geometric decoration.
* The Esquire range designed by Russel Wright (see p.169), with modern coupé shapes, pastel glazes and delicate incised botanical decorations, was not a commercial success and was only made from 1956 to 1962.
* The series of collectors' plates issued with the Edwin M. Knowles China Company name in the early 1980s were not in fact made by the factory.

TAYLOR, SMITH & TAYLOR

*Lu-Ray dinnerware by Taylor, Smith & Taylor
1940s; value code I*

Identification checklist for Lu-Ray dinnerware
1. Does it have a simple, refined modern shape?
2. Does it have distinctive bud-like organic finials?
3. Is it a pastel colour -- yellow, green, blue, pink, or grey?
4. Is it made of semi-porcelain?
5. Is it marked?

Taylor, Smith & Taylor
Founded in 1899 in Chester, West Virginia, the pottery produced semi-porcelain toilet ware, dinnerware, kitchenware, and specialities. Wares were made in a wide variety of shapes and patterns and were sold primarily through dime stores, mail-order catalogues, and as

premiums. The factory ceased trading in 1981 and is best known today primarily for a few keenly collected lines of tableware.

Patterns
The pottery's wide range of decoration included traditional transfer-printed scenic and ornamental patterns, and several printed patterns that mimicked European porcelain, French Haviland-type pastel flowery patterns, and French provincial ceramics such as Quimper Ware.
* Popular patterns were used on more than one shape line.
* The Silhouette or Taverne pattern shown on the bowl left, made in the 1930s, was used on Vogue, St Denis, and Laurel shapes. It was based on Hall China's popular Taverne pattern but is more easily found than Hall's version.
* In the 1930s and '40s floral transfer-printed patterns were a staple for dime-store trade. Most were unnamed and many had gold filigree borders.
* Most collectors concentrate on shape lines, which are easier to identify. Vistosa and Lu-Ray (main picture) are popular.
* Pebbleford (1950–60), p.157 right, is one of the most popular patterns.

156

Vistosa

Introduced in 1938 and produced into the early 1940s, Vistosa was the company's somewhat late contribution to the solid-colour casual dinnerware produced by manufacturers such as Bauer (see p.131) and Homer Laughlin (see p.136). It is now one of its most collectable lines.
* Vistosa had a more refined overall shape than other simpler California-style wares and featured a pie-crust rim.
* It was produced in mix-and-match brilliant green, blue, yellow, and red.
* Most standard forms were available, including plates, soup bowls, cups and saucers, cream jugs and sugar bowls, teapots, water jugs, salt and pepper pots, and egg cups. A sauce boat was added later.

Lu-Ray

Produced between 1938 and 1955, the Lu-Ray shape was assembled from the earlier flatware shapes of the Laurel line (1933) and the hollowware shapes of the 1936 Empire line.
* It was originally made in the four colours shown in the main picture – Windsor Blue, Surf Green, Persian Cream (yellow), and Sharon Pink – and a fifth colour, Chatham Grey, was added in 1948.
* Colours are glossier on earlier pieces and become increasingly matt through the 1940s.
* A distinctive feature was the organic bud-like finials, seen on the salt and pepper pots above.
* Lu-Ray is keenly collected today.

Other shapes

Two other popular shapes were created in the 1950s. The Versatile line, with a plain round coupé shape, was designed by John Gilkes and produced until the mid-1960s.
* It was issued with a variety of different decorative treatments including solid uniform pastel colours, bright litho-printed decorations with air-brushed edges, and stylish patterns with formal gold- and platinum-lined rims.
* The most popular Versatile finish was the Pebbleford speckled single-colour textured glaze, shown on the versatile dish below.
* Colours included Burnt Orange, Granite Gray, Honey,

Mint Green, Pink, Sand, Teal, Turquoise, Sunburst Yellow and Marble White. Mint Green, Honey, and Burnt Orange, are the rarest.

The distinguished industrial designer Walter Dorwin Teague (1883–1960) created the Conversation range, made 1950–54.
* The square and streamlined shape seen on the plates above, made in the 1950s, was very popular at the time and is relatively easily found today.
* The Conversation line was issued in at least 16 patterns. Most commonly found is the King O'Dell pattern featuring a jack-in-the-pulpit flower.
* The Conversation plates, top, show the Day Lily (left) and an unnamed pattern.

Deldare Ware by Buffalo
1908–25; value codes H/I

Identification checklist for Deldare Ware

1. Does it have a sage green body?
2. Does it have complex transfer-printed decorations filled with hand-painting?
3. Is the decoration based on illustrations of colonial-revival subjects?
4. Are they in the Arts and Crafts style?
5. Is the piece marked?

Buffalo Pottery Company

Established in Buffalo, New York, in 1901, and still active, Buffalo's production from c.1918 was largely vitreous institutional ware (see p.164) and custom services. Early semi-porcelain wares included soap premiums and a range of now keenly collected artwares with distinctive decoration.

Artwares

* Between 1905 and 1909 Buffalo made a wide variety of collectable pitchers with transfer-printed and filled decorations ranging from traditional Imari patterns to Art Nouveau. Many featured historical or fictional characters.
* The expensive Deldare Ware (1908–25), above, had a sage green body and complex transfer-printed decoration filled with colour by hand. The Arts and Crafts-style illustrations by Ralph Stuart included thematic series such as the Fallowfield Hunt, Ye Olden Days, and Dr Syntax. It was discontinued due to its cost and the limited market.

* Emerald Deldare, identified by a special mark and a lot of green in the decoration, was produced for one year only, in 1911.

Custom wares

* Among the most collectable custom wares are the service plates made for the Chesapeake and Ohio Railroad in 1932, featuring a Gilbert Stuart portrait of George Washington.
* The Roycroft service, which was made for the Roycrofters, a small Arts and Crafts-style colony in East Aurora, New York, and featured the insignia (shown on the Roycroft cup and saucer below, c.1910) used on their books, furniture, and metalwork.

METLOX POTTERIES

Aztec pattern Free-Form covered vegetable dish by Metlox 1950s; value code I

Identification checklist for Free Form tableware
1. Does it have an innovative modern form?
2. Does it have bold, graphic decoration?
3. Does it have an extreme 1950s style?
4. Is it marked?

Metlox Potteries
The pottery was founded in 1927 in Manhattan Beach, California, to produce ceramic signs. In 1934 Metlox began to produce tableware, kitchenware, and a range of figurines, vases, and novelties. The company's extensive range of cookie jars (see p.161) was introduced in 1959 and produced until the pottery closed in 1989. Metlox bought the Vernon Kilns' name and moulds in 1958, and produced Vernon Ware in a separate division.

Wares
* Early ranges include the brightly coloured California Poppy casual ware, Poppytrail tableware, and kitchenware, all launched in 1934.
* Mission Bell pastel-coloured tableware and kitchenware was made from 1935 to 1938 for Sears, Roebuck & Co.
* In the mid-late 1930s Metlox produced the Yorkshire range, based on English Staffordshire ware.
* From 1934 Carl Romanelli designed a range of animal figurines and novelties, and the Modern Masterpieces line that included figures, busts, wall pockets, book-ends, both figural vases, and vases with relief figures.
* The exotic Free Form tableware, seen above with the bold, graphic Aztec pattern, was one of the decorated lines introduced after WWII. Designed by Frank Irwin, the range included several extreme shapes, including a boomerang-shaped relish dish and attenuated beverage servers.
* Frank Irwin also designed the radical Mobile line for Metlox in the 1950s.
* Other important designers include Bob Allen and Mel Shaw, Harrison McIntosh, and Helen Slater.

Collecting
The most collectable Metlox ranges include the designs by Carl Romanelli, and the innovative Free Form and Mobile tableware ranges created by Frank Irwin.

Marks
* After 1934, Poppytrail was used, with or without Metlox (see below).

159

ONONDAGA POTTERY

Onondaga trade catalogue; 1937; value code I (per item)

Identification checklist for Onondaga 1930s Ware
1. Is it a piece of dinner or hotel ware?
2. Does it have a vitreous china body?
3. Does it have a white or tan body?
4. Is it decorated with hand-painting and hand-lining, or decal or print patterns?
5. If hotel ware, does it have a narrow moulded rim with a broad, deep well?
6. Is it marked Syracuse China?

Wares
Founded in 1871 in Syracuse, New York, and still active, Onondaga Pottery specializes in dinner and hotel ware (see p.165). From 1895 Syracuse China was used in the backstamp as the trade name for the improved vitreous-china body that was used exclusively from 1897.
* Mayflower, introduced c.1910, was the signature dinnerware shape.
* In 1927, new body colours were introduced: Old Ivory was used on the Mayflower shape but was soon used exclusively on Winchester. The Adobe tan body, shown above, was used from 1932 to 1972.
* The Marathon plate right (1926) is a good example of the

stylish custom and stock patterns Onondaga produced for their institutional customers.
* Exceptional examples of the technical and design skills include the service plates of the Mayflower Hotel range and Missouri-Pacific Railroad (1946–61).

COOKIE JARS

*Chilly Willie cookie jar by Nelson McCoy
1950s; value code H*

Identification checklist for McCoy cookie jars
1. Is it made of moulded stoneware or earthenware?
2. Does it have whimsical, novel shape?
3. Is it hand-painted, often in bright colours?
4. Is it functional, i.e. does it have a separate cover or lid?
5. Is it marked?

Cookie jars
Many American manufacturers produced cookie jars, either as an independent range or as part of their kitchenware lines. These cheerful containers are a popular collecting niche in the United States, where their manufacture over a long period offers virtually a history of popular motifs. They are available in a huge variety of colours, shapes, and designs, and most collectors look in particular for originality, charm, and humour, favouring the more extreme and bizarre designs, and collecting by subject and style rather than by maker.

Manufacturers
* The Nelson McCoy (see p.153) range, made from 1940 to 1990, was the company's major product. Early examples resembled pre-war kitchenware with geometric shapes and floral decoration; fruits were popular in the 1940s and '50s; early

American, rustic, cowboy, and Wild West themes were used in the 1960s; and an Apollo Moon Mission jar was made in the 1970s.
* The Chilly Willy cookie jar above was made with a red, blue, or yellow scarf. The many other animal character jars include Hocus the Rabbit, Mr and Mrs Owl, Gray Rooster, and Timmy Tortoise.
* The most keenly collected McCoy designs include Baseball Boy, Teddy Bear, Dog House, Jack O'Lantern, Cookies, Mother Goose, and Mammy (hands on stomach). * Watch out for fake Mammy cookie jars with the McCoy mark.
* Novelty jars are always popular and command a premium; the more traditional geometric kitchenware lines are less expensive
* Other major manufacturers include Red Wing Potteries (see p.140) and Metlox (see p.159).

KITCHENWARE

Canisters by Hull Pottery
1920–30: value code I

Identification checklist for American kitchenware
1. Is it made of stoneware or earthenware?
2. Is it thickly potted?
3. Does it have a thick, perhaps yellow, glaze?
4. Does it have a robust traditional form?
5. Does it have a thick roll-over rim?
6. Does it have simple decoration? Perhaps an embossed pattern or simple painted coloured bands?

Kitchenwares
In the late 19th to early 20thC, the burgeoning Ohio potteries such as the Hull Pottery made huge quantities of traditional kitchenware, including a wide variety of bowls, rectangular and oval baking dishes, pitchers or jugs in various sizes, teapots, cookie jars (see p.161), custard

cups, pudding dishes, canisters or storage jars, colanders, spice jars, pie plates, etc. Much of this ware was sold through mass-

market department stores, variety stores, and through mail-order catalogues such as Sears, Woolworth's, Kresge's, and McCrory's, and the buyers for these chains had a major impact on both design and production.

From the late 1940s kitchens were redesigned to house labour-saving devices such as refrigerators, washing machines and dishwashers, and kitchenware producers adapted production to include colour-coordinated mix-and-match oven-to-table ware and dishwasher-proof bodies and glazes.

Decoration
Decoration of earlier pieces was usually simple. Many straight-sided items such as canisters and spice jars had embossed or moulded decoration of contents names and such typically

American motifs as wheat pattern, as seen in the canisters opposite right and the spice jar (1905–17), below left, both made by the Hull Pottery. This type of decoration also made the straight sides easier to grasp. Bowls

typically had thick roll-over rims, as seen on the example on p.162, made by the Weller Pottery in 1920–30, to make them easier to hold and stack, and to protect against chipping.
* Many items were decorated with simple coloured bands, often in blue, as shown on the Hull Pottery jugs below.
* Other wares were decorated with hand-painted motifs, such as flowers or the bluebirds shown on the spice jar above, made by the Brush-McCoy factory in 1920–30.
* With the development of more sophisticated printing techniques, later kitchenwares were increasingly decorated with litho-printed patterns.

Yellow wares
Earthenware of any body colour can be called yellow ware when covered with an opaque, yellow glaze. Typical yellow wares are inexpensive, utilitarian bowls used for preparing and storing

food, such as the kitchenware bowls made by the Ohio potteries.
* Yellow ware is very rarely marked, and, although it is widely collected, examples are fairly common, typically plain, and affordable.

Collecting
Kitchenware was produced in large quantities so is readily available but good condition is essential, especially as many collectors want to be able to use the pieces they acquire.
* Shape, decoration, and condition are usually more important than manufacturer.
* More unusual items such as colanders are keenly collected.
* Always check for damage.
* Many canisters and spice jars were originally made in sets. Full sets are rarely found but can sometimes be built up over time.

* Many canisters and spice jars are now missing lids, which will reduce value.
* Decorated wares are generally more valuable than plain examples.
* Collectors may focus on one type of ware, such as jugs or spice jars, and collect many examples.

INSTITUTIONAL WARE

*Sterling China restaurant plate
1958; value code I*

Identification checklist for institutional ware
1. Is it made of vitreous china?
2. Is it heavily potted?
3. Is it sturdy and robust, with a thick rolled rim?
4. Is it decorated with a name or motif that identifies the institution?
5. Does it have underglaze decoration?

Designs and patterns
Institutional wares had to be robust. Typically they were thickly potted, with heavy-duty semi-vitreous or vitreous china bodies, with craze-resistant glazes, and sturdy damage-resistant rims, feet, and handles. Most were underglaze decorated with a transfer-printed central motif that identified the institution, as seen above, and a pattern or solid colour on the rim.
* Patterns tend to be traditional and conservative rather than to reflect new styles.
* More elaborate examples have all-over decoration or complex rim patterns.
* Illustrations of famous events or characters in American history, or indigenous North American Indians are keenly collected.

Mayer China Co. (1881–1989)
From 1915 Mayer made sturdy wares for famous hotels, transport companies, and institutions.

* The Bayberry plate (1950s), bottom left p.165, was produced exclusively for the Chalfonte-Haddon Hall in Atlantic City,

New Jersey. The mark typically includes the name of the range, manufacturer, retailer, and institution.
* The services for the Hotel DuPont in Wilmington, Delaware, featured a central motif that incorporated the DuPont name.
* The Indian Tree pattern was made as a stock design for distribution to many companies.

Sterling China Co. (1917–75)
Created specifically to make vitreous hotel china, Sterling was one of the leading manufacturers of hotel china and commissioned a range from Russel Wright (see p.169), whose design reflected the particular demands of institutional ware.
* Sterling patterns for the range included airbrushed stencils, solid colours, and decals.

Lamberton China
In 1923 Scammell China Co. bought Lamberton China and produced Lamberton's durable vitreous china under the Scammell name (see mark right). Scammell made wares for America's premier hotel, railway, and steamship companies.
* Most outstanding railway commission was the 1927 service for the centenary of the Baltimore and Ohio Railroad, with elaborate blue transfer designs that covered the surfaces.
* Lamberton service plates are among the finest US institutional china, with complex transfer-printed borders and pictorial

Washington's birth centennial in 1932, and the Wright Brothers' first flight.

Onondaga Pottery
The company's sturdy vitreous-china body (see p.160) was enhanced by several shape improvements specifically aimed at the institutional ware market.
* In 1897 the in-house designer Mark Haley introduced a round or rolled edge. Round Edge was immediately popular and was used for many years.
* In 1932 R. Guy Cowan introduced Econo-Rim, combining a narrow moulded rim with a broader, deeper well that contained juices, while using a smaller diameter and saving tray and table space.

* Econo-Rim changed the basic shape of hotel ware in the 1930s and soon became a standard shape.
* Syracuse China produced custom and stock patterns for a large number of institutions.
* Onondaga/Syracuse hotel, restaurant, and service plates are often collected for the wide variety of images that refer to people and events in contem-porary American life and American history. The Hotel Blackhawk plate shown above features an illustration of a Native American Indian.

devices. The design on the Daniel Boone hotel service plate, bottom p.164, was intended to show the development and colonization of the North American continent.
* Other patriotic motifs included the Mayflower, George

EVA ZEISEL

Museum dinnerware by Eva Zeisel for Castleton China late 1940s; value codes H/I (individual items)

Identification checklist for Eva Zeisel dinnerwares
1. **Does it have an organic, modern shape?**
2. **Is the design elegant?**
3. **Does it have unusual features, such as integral or tear-drop shaped handles?**
4. **Is the decoration solid-colour, or a pattern that enhances the form?**

Eva Zeisel (b.1906)
Born in Budapest, Eva Zeisel worked in Hungary, Germany, and Russia before moving, in 1938, to New York, where she worked as a teacher and free-lance designer of ceramics. Together with Russel Wright, she was largely responsible for interpreting the New Look organic freeform in ceramics in the 1940s, spearheading the new style both in the United States and in Britain (largely through her influence on Midwinter, see p.95) with a range of highly

influential classic modern designs that are eagerly collected.

Museum dinnerware
The 1940 Organic Design in Home Furnishings Exhibition in the Museum of Modern Art,

New York, prompted the director of Castleton China to ask the Museum to recommend a designer for a modern-style dinner service. MOMA recommended Zeisel but insisted on approving each piece, and the Museum service, designed c.1943, was finally launched to critical acclaim at a special MOMA exhibition – *Modern China: New Designs by Eva Zeisel* produced by Castleton China – in April 1946.
* Museum, shown above, was the first freeform modern shape made in fine china.
* The modern yet elegant and formal shapes had organic curves and fluent, undulant rims.
* Initially MOMA insisted on a clear glaze over a cream body, but subsequently Castleton produced Museum with various decorative schemes, although none was designed by Zeisel.
* Castleton China was a trade name of Shenango China Co. (see mark right).

Hallcraft designs
Zeisel produced several successful designs for Hall China's Hallcraft range
* Tomorrow's Classic, designed

in 1949–50 and produced from 1952, was one of Zeisel's most popular dinner services. The organic earthenware shapes, which included oval dinner plates, and distinctive, almost penguin-like salt and pepper shakers, had cheerful modern decoration.

* Tomorrow's Classic was designed with a white glaze but Hall insisted on patterns, which Zeisel and her assistants created. They included Frost Flowers, Buckingham (a calligraphic gate motif), and Fantasy, based on Naum Gabo-inspired parabolas, and colourful abstract designs such as Arizona and Dawn.

* In late 1954, a 20-piece Tomorrow's Classic line of ovenproof cookware and kitchen accessories was introduced. It included elegant, sculptural refrigerator jars, in matt seal

brown and white glazes, and recessed indented handles moulded into the body. The lids were sometimes decorated.

* The Century dinner service, designed in 1956, had graceful tear-drop shapes, with somewhat fragile handles, as shown on the bowl (1956) left p.166, with the Fern transfer-printed pattern. Although difficult to produce because of its attenuated shape, it was extremely practical, because it could be stacked and nested so easily.

* Tomorrow's Classic and Century are still available and affordable.

Town and Country
Designed in the mid-1940s, the Town and Country earthenware line was created for Red Wing Potteries (see p.141). It was modern, colourful, sturdy, and useful. The elegant formality of Museum was replaced by informal, biomorphic, slightly asymmetrical shapes, seen on the marmites (mid-1940s) above, with their innovative integral handles.

* Pieces included a bean pot, various bowls, casseroles, jugs, plates, relishes and platters, ashtrays, a cream jug and sugar bowl, teapot, sauce dish, cup and saucer, soup tureen, cruet, mug, and Lazy Susan.

* The salt and pepper shakers, with rounded sculptural nestling shapes, are very sought after by collectors. The other distinctive shape is the pitcher, with a flaring sculptured handle and lip.

* The deeply saturated and very modern glaze colours were produced in both matt and glossy finishes. They included Chalk White, Chartreuse, Dusk Blue, Forest Green, Metallic Brown, Peach, Rust, and Sand.

Other designs
In 1954 the Western Stoneware Company commissioned Zeisel to design a blue spongeware line.

* The new line included 50 new shapes, the most interesting of which are the bird-shaped casserole, sauce boat, and teapot.

* The 15 new patterns included solid-colour designs and hand-decorated designs in blue on white bodies.

* In the late 1950s and '60s, most of Zeisel's clients were German, Italian, and Japanese. Rosenthal commissioned the popular Eva porcelain dinner service (c.1958).

167

RUSSEL WRIGHT

*American Modern tableware by Russel Wright for Steubenville
1950s; value codes H/I (individual items)*

Identification checklist for American Modern
1. Does it have a modern streamlined shape?
2. Is it decorated in solid colours?
3. Is it sturdy and functional, with a casual style?
4. Is it marked?

Russel Wright (1904–76)
Russel Wright was one of the
leading freelance ceramic
designers in the US from the
1930s to the 1950s. He produced
tableware lines for a number
of large companies, but his
reputation was established with
American Modern, shown above,
probably the most popular
dinnerware ever made in the US,
selling over 125 million pieces
by the mid-1950s. Its success
was due to the modern design,
innovative marketing, and clever
packaging, which allowed
customers to begin with less
expensive small starter sets
rather than have to buy a whole
service, and encouraged them
to come back and add to their
collection over time. In 1951 the
Highlight line (1948–53)
he designed for Paden City
received both the Museum of
Modern Art's Home Furnishings
Award and the Trail Blazer
Award of the Home Furnishings
League. Wright's designs and
marketing strategies were widely
imitated.

American Modern
This streamlined, casual,
functional solid-colour wear,
seen above, was produced by
the Steubenville Pottery from
1939 to 1959 and was particularly
popular in the 1950s, when the

trend for informal entertaining
became established. It inspired
numerous copies, including the
British Studio range by Meakin
(see top p.12).
* Accessories included a covered
butter dish, salad bowl, round
relish tray, covered pitcher, and
salt and pepper shakers.
* Colours included Granite Grey,
Seafoam, Cantaloupe, Cedar
Green, Coral, White, Bean
Brown, Glacier Blue, Black,

Chutney, and Steubenville Blue.
* The streamlined design was
also very functional: casseroles,
such as the one seen above,
had integral single handles
(a ground-breaking feature also

used by Eva Zeisel, see p.167), and lids had solid knob handles that were easy to grasp.
* Because so many pieces were made – and of course used and so subject to everyday wear – condition is crucial to value.

Casual China
Complaints about the fragility of American Modern encouraged Wright to find a high-fired vitreous china body for his second tableware range, which he hoped to market as oven-to-table ware. The result was the Casual China range for Iroquois China Co. (see p.148), introduced in 1946 and popular throughout the 1950s.
* The sculptural yet functional forms, derived from the coupé shape, were smooth and modern, with a soft, almost melting quality, as seen on the jug and bowl shown below.
* The speckled solid-colour

glazes were available in mix-and-match colours that included Sugar White, Lemon Yellow, Ice Blue, Nutmeg, Avocado Yellow, Parsley Green, Oyster, Charcoal, Ripe Apricot, Pink Sherbet, Lettuce Green, Cantaloupe, Aqua, and Brick Red.
* Transfer-printed decoration was added from 1959.

Other designs
In 1948 Wright was commissioned by Sterling China Company (see p.165), a leading maker of hotel ware, for a new line. The result, shown on the leaf-patterned plate above right, c.1950, was both pleasing and useful.
* The plate was shaped to roll gently upwards from the bottom and curl under at the outer rim to provide greater strength and make it easier to grip.
* The solid colours – Ivy Green, Straw Yellow, Suede Grey, Cedar Brown, Shell Pink, and White – were approved by Wright, although Sterling designed individual patterns (see p.165).

* Much of this ware is not marked and only identified by the shapes and colours.

The White Clover line
Produced by Harker Pottery (see p.151) from 1953 to 1958, the White Clover dinnerware line is one of the least collectable of Wright's designs. Of more interest to today's collector is the General Electric ceramic clock that came as a companion piece. It was made in four colourways: Meadow Green, Coral Sand, Charcoal, and Golden Spice, shown on the clock below, made in the 1950s.

Esquire
The Esquire line designed for Edwin M. Knowles (see p.155) had elegant coupé shapes and pastel glazes with incised botanical decorations. Produced from 1956 to 1962, it was popular with store buyers but not with the general public, who found it costly compared with foreign wares readily available to them.

CONTINENTAL CERAMICS

The style and development of Continental ceramics in the 20thC reflects the diverse histories and traditions of the countries involved. While much of Europe had been shut down creatively during WWII, Scandinavia had continued to develop, and the small number of major factories and designers led to the development of a recognizable Scandinavian style, with factories such as Gustavsberg and Rorstrand in Sweden, Figgioflint and Stavangerflint in Norway, Arabia in Finland, and Nymølle and Royal Copenhagen in Denmark playing major roles. The inspiration for the Scandinavian style was often the organic forms of the native flora and fauna, which were interpreted both in shapes and in flat, graphic, often abstract patterns that were applied both to textiles and ceramics. A touring exhibition of Scandinavian art to the US and Canada in the 1950s firmly established the Scandinavian style that influenced ceramic design throughout Europe and the US in the 1950s and '60s.

In Italy, by contrast, the myriad local traditions and small producers defied a unified and cohesive Italian style. The post-WWII design boom and the use of coloured plastics resulted in equally brightly coloured and exuberant shapes and decoration in ceramics, which, although often un-marked, can be recognized by their style and flair, or, alternatively, by their often opulent design that at times transcended considerations of quality or price. Major designers included Piero Fornasetti (see p.35) and Marcello Fantoni, while the Richard-Ginori factory commissioned designs from the architect Gio Ponti.

German manufacturers were severely affected by both World Wars. In the 1920s and '30s, the tradition of high-quality porcelain, skilled modelling, and hand-painting was applied to fashionable forms, such as popular Art Deco figures and wall masks, by Goldscheider, Goebel, and Rosenthal (Bohemian factories often produced similar pieces but of medium quality and with prices to match), and Bauhaus-inspired ranges of well-designed mass-produced table- and domestic wares. Post-WWII, German and Austrian factories maintained their pre-war tradition of good quality, design, and workmanship, and commissioned tableware designs from distinguished designers worldwide. West German factories also produced ranges of cheap and cheerful ornaments for world export.

French ceramicists and designers launched hugely influential new styles, from Art Nouveau at the turn of the century, to the Art Deco style of the 1920s and '30s, and, in 1947, Christian Dior's hourglass-shaped New Look inspired a whole range of new organic ceramic forms. Leading manufacturers such as Sèvres and traditional centres such as Limoges adapted porcelain production to reflect new styles while maintaining their traditional ranges.

*Vase by Bjørn Wiinblad for Rosenthal
1960s; value code G*

Identification checklist for Bjørn Wiinblad ceramics
1. Does it have a tinted grey body?
2. Is it decorated with highly detailed busy line illustrations?
3. Does the decoration include foliage or check patterns?
4. Are the illustrations in pink, blue, green, brown, or black?
5. Is it signed?

Scandinavian style
Bjørn Wiinblad's designs for the Danish Nymølle factory represent the decorative, graphic side of Scandinavian style. They included modelled figural items, wall plaques, ceramic boxes, pendants, and other decorative items, and some highly collectable limited-edition studio pieces.

Decoration
The richly detailed illustrations were produced using copper-plate engraved transfer prints created by Wiinblad from 1946 to 1956 for Nymølle.
* All Nymølle pieces have a grey-tinted earthenware body: the Rosenthal vase above has

been stained grey to imitate the Nymølle look.
* Shapes tend to be simple, with clean lines. Wall plaques often have the typical popular Scandinavian design, softened square shape.
* The combination of highly graphic illustrative style applied to simple shapes was a typical feature of contemporary Scandinavian design and was widely imitated by European factories.
* Most Wiinblad pieces are signed on the back. Some earlier Nymølle pieces have a flamboyant script signature; a facsimile of this signature was also used in conjunction with the Rosenthal mark (see p.177).

SCANDINAVIAN II

*Tureen by Figgjo Fajansefabrik
1950s; value code I*

Identification checklist for Scandinavian kitchenware
1. Does it have a vitrified body?
2. Are the forms functional but decorative,
and modern in style?
3. Does it have decoration in bright or primary
colours?
4. Is the pattern graphic and abstract, or highly
stylized?
5. Does it have an overall cheerful appearance?

Gustavsberg
Stig Lindberg (1916–82) was
one of the designers who played
a major part in creating the
international reputation enjoyed
by the Swedish Gutavsberg
factory (est. 1825) in the 1950s.
He designed a range of wares
in highly influential shapes
and styles that epitomized the
fashionable Scandinavian style
and were widely copied
throughout Europe.
* His organic shapes and designs
were often inspired by Swedish
flora and fauna, for example the
signature Lov (leaf) dish below,
and naturalistic motifs, such as
the sycamore seed pods on the
vase below.

* Designs included playful, colourful freehand "folk-art"-style decoration on tin-glazed earthenware, or smaller, abstract, linear patterns.
* The curling leaf-shaped vessels of the 1950s, decorated with bands of colour, hand-painted in a style similar to that used on early tin-glazed maiolica, inspired, among others, Carlton Ware's range (p.58) of leaf-shaped decorative pieces, the decorating technique used by Rye Pottery on their tin-glazed earthenwares (see p.101), and 1950s Poole wares (see p.65).
* His Domino range of precise angular shapes with black-and-white geometric decoration, made in the late 1950s, anticipated the Op Art Movement of the 1960s.
* Lindberg's designs are marked with a distinctive hand-painted hand print (see bottom p.172) and are eagerly collected.

Rorstrand

The Swedish Rorstrand ceramic factory was committed to modern design, and its Picknick tableware range won awards at three Milan Triennales in the 1950s and early '60s.
* Designed by Marianne Westman (b.1935), Picknick was first produced in 1956.
* The functional, stylish, and durable shapes were decorated with a printed pattern of brightly coloured fruit, herbs, and vegetables, shown whole and sliced, as seen on the jam pot below.
* The pattern was printed in black and then hand-coloured and the main colour matched, where appropriate, with a solid colour lid.

Other manufacturers

The distinctive Scandinavian style became particularly popular and influential in the 1950s and early '60s.
* The Norwegian Figgioflint factory produced highly decorative and functional ranges. Many transfer-printed patterns featured figures – either at work

and play – or with a strongly mythical feel derived from Scandinavian folklore, sources that also inspired the work of the Danish designer Bjorn Wiinblad (see p.171). Others, such as the casserole in the main picture, were decorated with brightly coloured abstract designs.
* The Arabia factory (est. 1873) dominated ceramic production in Finland in the 1950s, producing the Kilta mix-and-match tableware service (1953–74), and playful designs such as a distinctive black-and-white *sgrafitto* decanter modelled as a man wearing a hat, and a series of ashtrays with detailed and humorous line illustrations reminiscent of Wiinblad's work, as seen in the ashtray above made in the 1950s.
* Throughout the 1960s the Danish Royal Copenhagen factory produced an extensive range of Fajance artware that was widely exported. The Royal Copenhagen Marselis vases are particularly popular.

Collecting

* Scandinavian ceramics were of a high quality and were widely sold by avant-garde stores such as Heal's in London. They were relatively expensive when new and have retained their value but can still be found unrecognized in Britain.
* The better pieces by Stig Lindberg and Royal Copen-hagen are rarely available.

*Terracotta face mask by Goldscheider
1930s; value code F*

Identification checklist for Goldscheider face masks
1. Is it made of terracotta?
2. Is it hand-painted in bold colours – red, yellow, green, or black?
3. Is it a well-modelled, elongated, highly stylized female face?
4. Does it have stylized, often pierced, eyes?
5. Does it have elaborately modelled curly hair or ringlets?
6. Is it marked?

Face masks
Manufacturers such as Goldscheider (1885–1953), Goebel, and Royal Dux made finely modelled, high-quality and very collectable Art Deco face masks.
* Goldscheider's series of six or more designs included some Negro studies.
* European copies of Goldscheider masks are difficult to differentiate from originals, so buy from a reputable dealer.
* Masks marked "Goldscheider made in England" were made by Myott & Co, who bought the rights to reproduce Goldscheider figures in the late 1930s.
* Goebel made full face, profile, and (very sought after) versions with two faces in profile looking at each other. All are marked with an impressed company.

mark and model number.
* Royal Dux masks include men, and a range based on the armed services.

Figures

Skilful modelling and top-quality hand-painting were also features of German and Austrian moulded, hand-painted porcelain figures. These typically depicted highly stylized modern young women in boldly coloured costumes, and elegant poses that celebrated their new-found freedom.
* Katzhutte figures are finely modelled with well-painted

expressive faces. All feature the company mark. The dancing girl came in a variety of poses, and sometimes with a pet. The dancing girl and the version with a borzoi are particularly popular.
* Goebel figures are rare and correspondingly valuable. The bases are impressed with a model number: a written mark was used on later figures. The sinuous lines of the girl with a lyre (early 1930s) shown below

is typical of their production.
* Goldscheider's Butterfly Girl, made in three sizes, is one of the

most keenly collected Art Deco figures. Most Goldscheider figures are marked underneath with the date, model number and company stamp.
* Other Goldscheider designs include dancing couples in contemporary dress, ballerinas, and Pierrettes from the *commedia dell'arte*.
* Rosenthal figures are marked on the base with the company mark and an impressed number. The Art Deco maiden (1920s) below shows off the company's fine porcelain.

Collecting

* Check all face masks for damage to vulnerable details

such as moulded hair and hair decorations.
* Art Deco figures are widely collected, especially those in "Jazz Age" poses.
* Good condition is essential. Check for restoration: tell-tale signs are subtle changes in skintone and glaze; or unusual hand-painted details like necklaces or bracelets that could mask joins.

G E R M A N

Lemonade set by Thomas
1960s; value code H

Identification checklist for 1960s German tableware
1. Is it made of high-quality porcelain?
2. Does it have a fashionable cylinder shape?
3. Does it have printed on-glaze decoration?
4. Does the decoration reflect contemporary styles, such as psychedelic patterns or bright colours with motifs inspired by textile designs?

German manufacturers
By the mid- to late 1950s many West German manufacturers had finished rebuilding after the war, and throughout the late 1950s and early 1960s were producing ranges of high-fashion tableware, much of which was exported.

Other potteries mass-produced a range of cheap and cheerful ornaments with contemporary decoration that were widely exported throughout Europe. Much of the fashionable ware in the 1950s and '60s had an element of hand-painting. The black 1950s vase with coloured decoration shown right is typical: it was decorated using a resist technique, hand-coloured and then finished in black.
* Typical decoration included crescents, plaids, and multi-coloured stripes.
* Such pieces are liable to flake but the quality of the design often outweighs minor flaws.
* Identification is difficult as they were often only back-stamped "Foreign".
* Forms varied widely, but typical colour combinations included black and yellow, or black with another contrasting colour or colours.
* Unmarked pieces, or those by little-known factories, are more accessibly priced but should be in good condition,

in a fashionable style and preferably hand-finished for maximum value – the word "handarbeit" means handcrafted.

Domestic wares

In the 1960s, Goebel, well-known for its fine 1930s range of figures and face masks (see pp.174–75), was producing table and domestic wares in the newly fashionable cylinder shapes and bright patterns.
* The 1960s oil and vinegar bottle and jam pot shown below are decorated with popular contemporary boldly drawn and coloured motifs of everyday items.
* The printed decoration, which draws heavily on textile design, is of very good quality, which is reflected in the value.

* Goebel produced several variations on these domestic patterns.

In the 1970s, Villeroy & Boch launched the Avant Garde collection, an inspired design that included the La Boule dinner service shown right.
* Designed by Helen von Boch (b.1938) it comprised 19 pieces that fitted together, one inside the other, to form a ball-shaped sculpture for the sideboard.
* Launched in 1971, the colours anticipated the fashionable 1970s earthy palette.
* Such pieces are now eagerly collected as prime examples of the German tradition of innovative design established by the Bauhaus.

Rosenthal

In the 1950s Rosenthal maintained its reputation for high-quality porcelain and design, commissioning modern ranges from European and American designers.
* The New Look-inspired range designed by Beate Kuhn (b.1927), introduced 1955, consisted of extravagantly shaped vases, many with patterns inspired by Miró paintings.
* Around 1957–58, Eva Zeisel (see p.166) designed the very successful Eva tableware range.
* The Danish designer Bjørn Wiinblad (see p.171) created illustrated series, dated plates,

fancies, and teaware ranges.
* In 1952 Raymond Peynet (see p.41) designed a successful giftware range.
* The celebrated American industrial designer Raymond Loewy (1893–1986) and Richard Latham (b.1920) created the "2000" service, with its highly fashionable curving hour-glass shapes, in 1954.
* The Rosenthal Studio Line, introduced 1961, included ornamental artware by such notable figures as the Finnish designer Tapio Wirkkala (1915–85) and the British sculptor Henry Moore (1898–1986).

FRENCH

*Primavera enamelled vase
1920s; value code E.*

Identification checklist for Primavera hand-made ceramics
1. Is it made of earthenware?
2. Does it have a simple, sculptural, and perhaps avant-garde shape?
3. Does it have enamelled decoration?
4. Is the decoration stylized?
5. Is it signed?

Sèvres
Under Georges Lechevallier-Chevignard, Sèvres produced high-quality Art Deco wares at the 1925 Paris Art Deco Exhibition, and displayed vases and tablewares in Neo-classical forms but with elaborate stylized Art Deco decoration, often enhanced with gilding.
* Sèvres Art Deco pieces are now highly collectable, especially those by top designers such as Suzanne Lalique (b.1899), Jacques Emile Ruhlmann (1879–1933), and Jean Dupas (1882–1964).
* Sèvres responded to the demand for fashionable ceramic animal sculptures. These included finely modelled pieces such as the gazelle top, p.179, in typically Deco colours.
* The ceramic vase right, designed in 1950 and decorated by Pierre-Auguste Gaucher in

1952, has a typically elegant Sèvres form and decoration incorporating gilding.

Limoges

Many Limoges factories created notable Art Deco pieces. Theodore Haviland & Cie (est.1797) commissioned designs from Suzanne Lalique and Raoul Dufy.

* Lalique designed plates depicting grapes and vines in a typical Deco palette of black, silver, and green.
* Dufy decorated wares with brightly coloured floral and foliage motifs.
* Jean Luce designed a tableware range decorated with Art Deco motifs such as angular sunbursts, zigzags, and clouds.
* The playful duck-shaped tea and coffee service below, made c.1927, was designed by Edouard-Marcel Sandoz.

Primavera

Primavera, the design studio of the Au Printemps Parisian department store, produced a range of fine Art Deco ceramics, including figures, simple monochrome animal studies, and vases, either moulded, or, more desirable, hand-made and decorated by artists.

* Typically forms were relatively simple but original, with a sculptural quality.
* The earthenware tends to have a reddish tone, often with evidence of some gentle crazing, usually apparent from the inside.
* Moulded wares carry an incised signature.
* Hand-made artist-decorated wares, such as the vase in the main picture by Claude Levy,

have a hand-painted signature on the base.
* Well-known Primavera designers include Jean Jacques Adnet, Marcel Renard, and Leon Zack; decorators include Claude Levy, Colette Gueden, Charlotte Chaucet-Guillere, and Madeleine Saugez.
* Réné Buthaud (1886–1987), one of the leading French Art Deco ceramicists, designed highly collectable wares for Primavera, including bulbous-shaped vases and bowls, with painted, incised crackle-glazed decoration in brownish tones.

In the 1920s and '30s Longwy produced wares for Primavera, often with crackle-glazed grounds.

* The elongated pear-shaped Longwy vase above, probably made in the 1930s, has a bright palette of blue and yellow: other pieces had ivory-and-grey crackled grounds decorated with brown, black, and reddish tones.
* Longwy pieces have a printed maker's mark.

ITALIAN I

Lamp base by Marcello Fantoni
1950s; value code G

Identification checklist for Marcello Fantoni 1950s ceramics

1. Is it a sculptural shape?
2. Is the design inspired by mythological and historical imagery?
3. Does it have on-glaze coloured enamel decoration?
4. Is it hand-painted?
5. Does it have an individualistic style?

Workshops and manufacturers
The majority of Italian ceramics were produced in small workshops, and the range of shapes, styles, and decoration is as diverse as the many different makers and their regional traditions. In the 1950s potters explored contemporary art and made pieces with brilliant glazes, different textures, and Modernist decoration, and Italian potteries produced and exported large quantities of inexpensive, brightly decorated domestic ware in modern shapes. Many pieces were unmarked, but certain factories, such as the Faenzarella pottery in Vietri, had a distinctive style. Designs were changed on a regular basis so a great variety of patterns and shapes was produced. One of the best-known manufacturers was Richard-Ginori (see p.182).

Decoration
In the 1950s, the long Italian tradition of hand-painted pottery was influenced by the work of Pablo Picasso (see p.40), and many other artists and Italian ceramicists developed their own, highly individualistic styles that reflected their particular preoccupations.

* Marcello Fantoni (b.1915) created colourful, often sculptural ceramics, such as the lamp base with flaring sides shown in the main picture.
* The incised underglaze figure of a knight on horseback with on-glaze coloured enamel decoration reflects Fantoni's interest in mythological and historical imagery that emerged in his work during the 1950s.
* The Desimone jug below reflects Picasso's influence both

in the subject-matter (a clown) and the graphic treatment of the face.
* Desimone flask and other bottle-shaped forms were decorated with trailing outline illustrations and Picasso-style faces that were colour-infilled on the glaze before firing so the colours spread and blurred slightly.
* Piero Fornasetti (see p.35) was one of the leading exponents of surface decoration with a range of transfer-printed designs that were usually applied to blanks.

Texture

Guido Gambone (1909–69), founder of the Faenzerella

factory, explored the effects of texture, as seen on the thick bubbled glaze on the striped ug with the twisted handle shown bottom p.180.
* Even unsigned Faenzerella pieces can be identified by the use of texture combined with rich, bright colours, and a milky glaze over greyish clay.
* Texture was often added, as well as spots and other designs, to give added relief to designs.

Shapes

Italian potteries made daring shapes in the 1950s, ranging from highly impractical, but very decorative, curving asymmetric jugs and vases to the playful cheese boards shown below, made in the 1950s with hand-painted decoration.
* The rectangular cheese board with primary coloured stripes resembles an abstract canvas and is a good example of how quickly Italian ceramicists adapted fine art into decorative techniques.
* The wavy-edged illustrated cheese board is an example of the 1950s fashion for celebrating the enjoyment of food and newly restored domesticity. It is inscribed "Ceramica di Milano".

Collecting

The range and variety of Italian ceramics offers collectors an equally wide collecting choice, with prices to match.
* Marked pieces by Fornasetti, Fantoni or Gambone fetch quite large sums.
* Stylish, unmarked pieces will be more accessible.
* Inexpensive domestic ware is often chipped, and the glaze may be flaked or worn. However, very minor damage can be overlooked on a particularly good pattern or shape.
* Pieces with extravagant shapes, especially if grouped together to create a visual impact, are very collectable.

*Vase designed by Gio Ponti for Richard-Ginori
c.1925; value code F*

Identification checklist for Richard-Ginori ceramics
1. Is it made of porcelain?
2. Is it high quality?
3. Is it marked?
4. Does it reflect the decorative styles of its time in a distinctive way?
5. Does it have an architectural feel?

Richard-Ginori
In 1896 the family-owned Ginori porcelain factory in Doccia was incorporated with the Societá Richard of Milan and became known as Richard-Ginori Societá Ceramica Italiana.

In the early 20thC the company made some fine Art Nouveau and Art Deco pieces, and by the 1950s Richard-Ginori was one of the leading Italian ceramics manufacturers, producing tableware, vases, and urns painted with strongly stylized geometric patterns, architectural forms, figures, or drapery. These pieces reflect the decorative styles of the time,

By 1970 Richard-Ginori was a multi-factory operation, and the company continues to produce much of the best-quality porcelain in Italy.

Designers
The distinguished Italian architect Gio Ponti (1891–1979) worked for Ginori from 1923 to 1930, creating many different ceramic designs, including one-off art pieces such as the hand-painted porcelain vase in the main picture. His decorative pieces for Ginori won a prize at the Art Deco exhibition of 1925 in Paris. Giovanni Garibaldi (1908–71), artistic director at Ginori from 1947, helped develop the innovative Prospettive modern range created by industrial designers, that included, in 1954, a table service that stacked vertically into a column. Other designs produced by Garibaldi included tableware and tiles decorated with linear abstract patterns.

GLOSSARY

applied decoration surface ornament made separately and applied to the body of an object.

backstamp mark applied to the base of commercially made ceramic ware giving details of manufacturer.

basalt unglazed, very hard, fine-grained stoneware stained with cobalt and manganese oxides, developed by Wedgwood c.1768.

biscuit (bisque) unglazed porcelain or earthenware fired once only.

blank undecorated ceramic ware.

blue-and-white white ceramics with painted or printed cobalt-blue decoration.

body material from which a piece of pottery or porcelain is produced.

bone china soft-paste porcelain consisting of petuntse (china stone), kaolin (china clay), and calcined bone ash.

celadon semi-opaque, green-tinted glaze used first on ware made during the Chinese Sung Dynasty (960–1280).

china originally an alternative term for Chinese porcelain. Since the early 19thC the term has been used to refer to bone china or porcelain.

chinoiserie decoration consisting of Oriental-style figures and motifs, such as pagodas, pavilions, birds, and lotus flowers, that permeated Europe from the Far East; prevalent from the late 17thC.

chintzware ware decorated with an all-over, usually dense, floral pattern.

crackle glaze (craquelure) deliberate cracked effect achieved by firing ceramics to a precise temperature.

crazing tiny, undesirable surface cracks caused by shrinking or other technical defects in a glaze.

creamware cream-coloured earthenware with a transparent lead glaze, developed by Wedgwood c.1760.

earthenware type of pottery that is porous and requires a glaze.

litho (decal USA) multicoloured image printed onto paper backing sheet. When soaked in water, the image can be slid from the paper to the surface of the biscuit-fired ware.

Can be overglaze or underglaze.

eggshell porcelain type of slip-cast, razor-thin porcelain made in 19thC Japan and Europe.

enamel form of decoration involving the application of metallic oxides to metal, ceramics, or glass in paste form or in an oil-based mixture, which is then usually fired for decorative effect.

faience French term for tin-glazed earthenware.

firing process of baking ceramics in a kiln. Temperatures range from 800 to 1100°C (1500–2000°F) for earthenware to 1400°C (2550°F) for the second firing of hard-paste porcelain.

flambé glaze made from copper, usually deep crimson, flecked with blue or purple, and often faintly crackled (due to controlled reduction firing).

flatware term embracing all flat objects, such as plates and salvers.

gilding method of applying a gold finish to ceramics, or glass.

glaze glassy coating that gives a smooth, shiny surface to ceramics and seals porous ceramic bodies.

hard-paste porcelain also known as true porcelain. It was first made in China using the combination of kaolin (china clay: 50%), petuntse (china stone: 25%), and quartz (25%).

hollowware any hollow items such as bowls, teapots, jugs; distinct from flatware.

Imari Japanese porcelain with dense decoration, based on brocade patterns, in a palette that is dominated by underglaze blue, iron red, green, manganese, yellow, and gold.

incised decoration decoration that is cut into the body of an object with a sharp metal point.

intaglio carving type of carving whereby forms are sunken into, as opposed to being moulded on to a surface.

jardinière plant container made from a variety of materials, including glass, silver, or pottery.

jasper ware hard, fine-grained, coloured stoneware developed by Wedgwood in the 1770s.

kaolin (china clay) fine white granite clay used to make hard-paste porcelain.

lead glaze clear glaze generally composed of silicaceous sand, salt, soda, and potash, mixed with a lead component.

lustre ware pottery with an iridescent surface produced using metallic pigments, usually silver or copper.

majolica corruption of the term maiolica, which refers to a type of 19thC earthenware in elaborate forms with thick, brightly coloured glazes.

on-glaze any porcelain decoration painted in enamels or transfer-printed on top of a fired glaze.

parian semi-matt porcelain made with feldspar and therefore not requiring a separate glaze. Also called statuary porcelain, it became known as parian because of its similarity to the white marble from the Greek island of Paros.

pâte-sur-pâte type of ceramic decoration involving low-relief designs carved in layers of slip and resembling cameos.

piercing hand-cut patterns and decoration through the clay, before firing.

porcelain *see* soft-paste porcelain and hard-paste porcelain and bone china.

Queensware alternative name given by Wedgwood to its creamware made in honour of Queen Charlotte, who commissioned a creamware tea service from the company in 1765.

redware red-bodied ware, generally unglazed and often decorated with applied motifs in relief.

relief decoration decoration that stands out from the surface of any object and is usually described, according to its depth, as low-relief or high-relief.

reticulation intricate pierced decoration on thin walled porcelain.

salt glaze thin, glassy glaze applied to some stoneware and produced by throwing salt into the kiln at the height of firing. The glaze may show a pitted surface, known as "orange peel".

sang-de-boeuf brilliant red ceramic glaze developed in China in the early 18thC.

sgraffito form of ceramic decoration incised through a coloured slip, revealing the ground beneath.

slip smooth dilution of clay and water used in the making and decoration of pottery.

slip casting manufacture of thin-bodied ceramic ware and figures by pouring slip into a mould.

slip trailing application of slip to a ceramic form to decorate the surface.

slipware type of red-bodied earthenware decorated largely with slip in contrasting colours.

soft-paste porcelain (artificial porcelain) porcelain formula made from a range of ingredients, which may include soapstone or bone ash, but without the kaolin used in hard-paste porcelain.

sponging application, with a sponge, of colour or a glaze to a ceramic piece after firing, to produce a mottled appearance.

stippling technique of creating intricate painted designs on ceramics by applying dots of colour with the point of a brush.

stoneware type of pottery fired at a higher temperature than earthenware, making it durable and non-porous. May be covered in a salt glaze.

studio pottery pottery that has been individually designed and crafted.

terracotta lightly fired red earthenware, usually unglazed.

throwing the technique of shaping ceramic vessels by hand on a rotating wheel.

tin glaze glassy glaze made opaque by the addition of tin oxide and commonly used on earthenware.

transfer *see* transfer printing.

transfer printing the process of transferring a single-colour image (a transfer), printed from an engraved copper plate on to tissue paper, on to the unglazed surface of a ceramic object.

tube-lining type of ceramic decoration in which thin trails of slip are applied as outlines to areas of coloured glaze.

underglaze colour or design painted before the application of the glaze on a ceramic object. Blue is the most common underglaze colour.

white ware white porcelain which has been glazed but not decorated, or white-glazed domestic earthenware.